Breaking the Bonds of
EVIL

Breaking the Bonds of
EVIL

*How to Set People Free
from Demonic Oppression*

REBECCA GREENWOOD

Chosen
Grand Rapids, Michigan

Published by Chosen Books
a division of Baker Publishing Group
P.O. Box 6287, Grand Rapids, MI 49516-6287
www.chosenbooks.com

Printed in the United States of America

Library of Congress Cataloging-in-Publication Data
Greenwood, Rebecca, 1967-
    Breaking the bonds of evil : how to set people free from demonic oppression / Rebecca Greenwood.
        p.   cm.
    Includes bibliographical references and index.
    ISBN 10: 0-8007-9411-7 (pbk.)
    ISBN 978-0-8007-9411-8 (pbk.)
    1. Exorcism. 2. Demoniac possession. 3. Spirit possession. 4. Spiritual warfare. 5. Demonology. 6. Pastoral theology. I. Title.
BV873.E8G74 2006
235′.4—dc22   2006011645

Unless otherwise indicated, Scripture is taken from the HOLY BIBLE, NEW INTERNATIONAL VERSION®. NIV®. Copyright © 1973, 1978, 1984 by International Bible Society. Used by permission of Zondervan. All rights reserved.

Scripture marked AMP is taken from the Amplified® Bible, Copyright © 1954, 1958, 1962, 1964, 1965, 1987 by The Lockman Foundation. Used by permission.

Scripture marked CEV is taken from the Contemporary English Version © 1991, 1992, 1995 by American Bible Society. Used by permission.

Scripture marked KJV is taken from the King James Version of the Bible.

Scripture marked MESSAGE is taken from *The Message* by Eugene H. Peterson, copyright © 1993, 1994, 1995, 2000, 2001, 2002. Used by permission of NavPress Publishing Group. All right reserved.

Scripture marked NLT is taken from the *Holy Bible*, New Living Translation, copyright © 1996. Used by permission of Tyndale House Publishers, Inc., Wheaton, Illinois 60189. All rights reserved.

The information given in *Breaking the Bonds of Evil* is biblical, pastoral and spiritual in nature. It is not professional or medical counsel and should not be viewed as such. Rebecca Greenwood, Christian Harvest International and Chosen Books hereby disclaim any and all responsibility or liability for any adverse or damaging effects that may be asserted or claimed to have arisen as a result of use of this material.

Names of individuals and details about their lives have been changed throughout this book in order to protect their identities, but all stories are true.

To my three beautiful and precious daughters, Kendall, Rebecca and Katie. No words can ever express the joy you have brought into my life. You are each blessed with an exceptional spirit and perseverance, and exemplify a joyful and steadfast love. I can honestly say through your example, I learn from each of you daily. I love all three of you dearly and pray the Lord's best for each of your lives.

CONTENTS

This chapter defines the key aspects of deliverance ministry. Along with an overview of demonic oppression and influence, we ask the question, Who is the deliverance minister?

Jesus came not only to bring salvation to humankind but also to defeat the power of Satan and his demons. In this chapter we investigate Jesus' authority and the radical freedom people experienced as a result of the "power encounter" between light and dark.

Satan is the father of lies! He is a created being who fell from heaven. He is also the master and commander of demons. Who or what are these demons, and what is their purpose?

If Christians have victory in Jesus, how can demons possibly influence our lives? This seeming contradiction has left many Christians unprepared for the enemy's attempts to wreak havoc in our lives. We explore the tripartite nature of man and learn how demons use the Fall to their advantage.

5. Closing the Door on the Enemy   71

Scripture tells us that the enemy comes to kill, steal and destroy. We can be sure that if we open a door for him, he will walk through with evil intentions. In this chapter we discover a number of ways that we open doors—often without realizing it. This knowledge will help us shut out his efforts to imprison us physically, emotionally and spiritually.

6. Authority of the Believer   95

Jesus gives His followers powerful authority, but we often hesitate to take action or enforce obedience where demons are concerned. How can this be when we have influence over all the power of the enemy in Jesus' name? Here are three important guidelines that keep us focused on the mission and out of error.

7. Diagnosing Demons   107

In order to detect and expose satanic strategies, we need to know how to identify demons correctly. Here we uncover the identities and strategies of many of the demons encountered in deliverance ministry.

8. Setting the Stage for Ministry   131

Before initiating deliverance ministry, we need to gather specific information from the person seeking help. Is this really a deliverance issue? Is this individual saved? Is the person willing to cooperate with ministry leadership?

9. Team Ministry   145

Because it is based on corporate prayer and a wide range of gifts, team ministry is powerful and effective. We will discuss the responsibility of the leader, traps to watch out for and how the Lord works through prophetic revelation.

10. How to Conduct a Ministry Session   153

Now it is time to engage in effective deliverance ministry and set the captive free. We learn here how to conduct a ministry session from start to finish. Discussions also include dealing with demonic manifestations and the place of inner healing in deliverance ministry.

11. Walking in Freedom   177

Demons do not like to lose their hold on children of God. Once cast out, they will always try to regain entrance. Here are the final responsibilities of the deliverance minister, including the strategy of self-discipline and other key ingredients for securing freedom and victory.

FOREWORD

The Holy Spirit gives Christians many spiritual gifts. All 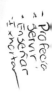 seven of the "motivational gifts" listed in Romans 12:6–8 are the duty of every Christian, but one of the gifts will represent the stronger motivating force in each person's life—either teaching, mercy, giving, service or one of the other three.

First Corinthians 12:7–10 lists nine "manifestation gifts," which are particularly evident in the context of ministry in the power of the Holy Spirit. Whether a word of wisdom, a word of knowledge, an unusual level of faith, gifts of healing or one of the other five, these are ways the Holy Spirit expresses His involvement in ministry.

At various ministry times and under various circumstances, a person will display one or another of these manifestation gifts. But Paul says clearly that "to one" and "to another" the Holy Spirit gives, as He decides. In other words, no one person will exhibit them all. Why not? Because God created us not to be a collection of "lone rangers," each doing his or her own thing, but to be an interdependent body of many members working together in symphony.

The third list of spiritual gifts, the "ministry gifts," is found in Ephesians 4:11: apostle, prophet, pastor (or, more accurately, pastor/teacher), teacher and evangelist. Notice that these are four (or five, depending on how you count them) ministry offices that the Holy Spirit has given the Church.

Missing among each of these lists of gifts is "deliverance" or "deliverance minister." Why? Because regardless of the blessing that an anointed Christian proficient in deliverance brings to the Church, deliverance ministry is not an office. And regardless of the supernatural qualities of administering the deliverance of a demonized person, deliverance is a sign, not a gift. It is a sign of true discipleship.

Somehow the 21st-century version of Western Christianity has conveniently separated being a Christian from being a disciple. Most of us consider and refer to ourselves as Christians rather than as Christ's disciples. Why do we make that distinction? First, because *disciple* speaks of one who is disciplined. Americans rarely apply discipline to their Christian lives. Christianity has to fit into our free time; we rarely make time for it. Second, a disciple is one who has been trained to do what he or she does. Jesus told His disciples that not only would they do the works He did but they, too, would cast out demons. And they did! (See John 5:20 and Mark 16:17.)

Deliverance is not a spiritual gift, then, nor is a deliverance minister a church officer. Deliverance is the job of every Christian disciple!

Most books written on deliverance, frankly, are too long and too complicated, and they make the ministry of deliverance seem more than it is—or, worse, less than it is. Or they present deliverance as a mysterious ministry for the rare and uniquely gifted few. Jesus, on the other hand, taught deliverance ministry to common men. Their training? They had seen Him cast out demons. Then Jesus sent them out on their own to cast out demons themselves. And this was before the Holy Spirit had been sent at Pentecost to live inside them! (Jesus did, however, make special arrangements for them; see Luke 10:19.)

Our friend Rebecca Greenwood, who was reared a Methodist, then a Baptist, presents deliverance ministry in a clear-minded, practical, uncomplicated and theologically sound way. She is not a novice, nor does she practice strange methods. To her, deliverance is more than mere theory; it is proficiency. This book is a biblical perspective on the demonstrable fact that, through Becca's life and the lives of others, God still empowers and expects Christians to cast out demons today.

As the Church age draws to a close and the last great harvest of souls is reaped, disciples of Christ must be prepared to help those coming out of darkness to be freed from its clutches. This book needs to be widely read and taught.

Eddie and Alice Smith
U.S. Prayer Center
www.usprayercenter.org

ACKNOWLEDGMENTS

No book is possible without the help, assistance, mentoring and belief of others. There are numerous individuals who have made the writing of this book a reality. I would like to take this opportunity to acknowledge all of those who have impacted my life and made the writing of this book possible.

To Eddie and Alice Smith, thank you for the training and mentoring you have provided and continue to provide in my life. Alice, your belief in me and the years of ministering together have been the highlight of my Christian walk. Thank you for your love and support. You truly are a spiritual mother who is deeply loved and appreciated. Eddie, thank you for the coaching in writing and your father's heart of always being available. You have encouraged, stretched and caused me to go deeper and higher in the Lord. I believe and pray that the best is yet ahead for both of you. Thank you, faithful servants and leaders in Christ.

Peter and Doris Wagner, thank you for your pioneering, apostolic spirit. You are always the forerunners of the new thing to come, and speaking as one from the younger generation for whom you have pioneered, I say thank you from the bottom of my heart. What an incredible ministry and legacy you have given to the Body of Christ throughout the earth! I love you both.

To my mom and dad, thank you for always being there for me. Thank you for providing your home for me to accomplish the writing of the book. Yet again, you have shown me the sacrificial heart of a true mother and father. No matter what the age or the circumstance, you have always unyieldingly given and supported. No words can even express the gratitude and love I have for you. Thank you.

To my sister, Ronda. You have always been more than a sister: also a dear friend. Thank you for your love and encouragement and for always being there for me. I love you.

To my precious daughters, Kendall, Rebecca and Katie. No mom could ask for daughters more precious and sweet than you. As each day goes by, I thank the Lord for His faithfulness to you as you mature into beautiful young women. I have witnessed you in good times and bad, and I stand in awe of the perseverance and love that pours out of each of you. What a privilege to be your mother! I love you.

To my husband, what can I say? You have put up with the writing period of yet another book. You have encouraged and pressed me on toward the goal. Thank you for standing and loving me through the process. You are my biggest fan and cheerleader. I would not be here without you. I love you.

Thank You, Lord, yet again for the privilege to partner with You. What an awesome opportunity to see lives transformed for Your glory! You are a faithful Father, and every day that I wake to serve You is a true honor and joy. To You be all glory and honor and power forever!

INTRODUCTION

I will always remember the challenge I received from Alice Smith fifteen years ago. Her words still resound vividly in my mind: "Don't just sit on the pew and be a spectator. Submit yourself to a mentor and become an active participant in the army of God on the front lines!"

As Alice spoke those words to the ladies' Bible study group I was attending, my spirit leapt. I felt as if this challenge were spoken directly to me. After her talk, I approached Alice eagerly and said, "I want to submit myself to your leadership in order to be trained in deliverance ministry and spiritual warfare."

She replied with the wisdom of a mentor and an experienced practitioner of deliverance ministry. "Great!" she said. "I know you are ready, but your family as a whole has to be spiritually prepared before you become involved in deliverance ministry. Are they ready?"

I had never thought about this and was uncertain about our readiness as a group. She instructed me, first, to tell Greg, my husband, about my desire. "Tell Greg that you feel God is calling you to be involved in deliverance ministry," she said. "Submit this to him. Explain the necessity of your family's readiness before you begin praying at this level.

15

When he feels the timing is right, let me know." That was the moment I began to learn about deliverance ministry. Alice had begun the training process.

I did as she said and that evening told Greg about the calling I had received from the Lord to be involved in deliverance ministry. He responded in a positive and supportive manner and agreed to do as Alice had instructed.

Greg began to pray. Not only was he seeking direction from the Lord about the timing of this new venture, but he was also laying a prayer shield over our family.

Greg prayed for five weeks. During this time, I did not ask him for any progress reports. I entrusted my desire to be involved in this ministry to him and the Lord. Then one day Greg said to me, "Becca, we are ready."

I had so released this issue to him, I responded, "Ready for what?"

He smiled and reminded me, "Ready for you to begin training in deliverance ministry."

I was excited and called Alice.

No time was wasted. Within five days, Alice had enlisted me as a participant on a deliverance team. But as the day of my first deliverance ministry experience approached, I began to wonder what I had gotten myself into. What if something bizarre happened as we prayed? What if a demonic manifestation occurred? I was raised in churches that never talked about Satan and demons. My excitement soon began to dissipate and turned into nervousness. I fasted and prayed. "Please, Lord," I begged, "give me an anointing for this ministry. If a demon should manifest itself, help me not to run out of the room in fear!" Alice still says that she was not sure who was more nervous the day of ministry, me or the demons we were about to confront!

But God was faithful. I watched as He led the prayer ministry team through powerful encounters with darkness. Those demons did not stand a chance. Right before our eyes, the Lord began to move on behalf of that hurting individual and undo all the years of trauma and demonic influence. I was hooked. From that point forward, I became actively involved in deliverance ministry as a frontline participant. I discovered that my heart's desire is to help people understand that our awesome heavenly Father truly desires to set the captive free.

As I moved forward and matured in the call of deliverance ministry, my awareness of the needs around me also grew. In fact, I had a difficult time managing all the requests for ministry sessions. I began to train new teams in order to handle the demand on the ministry schedule.

Deliverance is an immense need and is generally missing in the Body of Christ, especially in the Western Church. I have traveled extensively to other nations of the world; many of them exhibit in-depth knowledge and understanding of the supernatural and the need for deliverance ministry. Churches in the United States are behind in this area. The good news is that God is changing this. Many believers are beginning to walk in their God-given authority to help those bound by darkness.

At this strategic time, it is my prayer that *Breaking the Bonds of Evil* will present you with the truth and value of deliverance ministry, and will equip pastors and laypeople alike to pray and see the captives set free. We need more deliverance ministers in the Body of Christ! Just as Alice Smith issued this challenge to me fifteen years ago, I offer it now to you as you read this book: "Don't just sit on the pew and be a spectator. Submit yourself to a mentor and become an active participant in the army of God on the front lines!" I assure you it will prove to be a decision you will not regret.

1

DELIVERANCE DEFINED

When evening came, they brought to Him many who were
under the power of demons, and He drove out the spirits
with a word and restored to health all who were sick.

Matthew 8:16, AMP

God desires that each of His children walk in victory and
freedom in all areas of our lives. The Fall of man made it
impossible, of course, for us to achieve this on our own.
Our spiritual communion with our heavenly Father was
broken, and we were destined for eternal separation from
Him. But God responded to our need out of His immense
love for us and sent His only Son to redeem us and save us
from destruction. Jesus Christ became the sacrifice for all
humankind, securing salvation for all who will hear and
respond to the truth of redemption through Him: "For God
so loved the world that he gave his one and only Son, that

whoever believes in him shall not perish but have eternal life" (John 3:16).

Accepting salvation through Jesus Christ is the ultimate spiritual decision. And when we make it, we begin a lifetime of spiritual transformation—of God guiding us, changing us, transforming our fallen nature into His likeness, leading us from glory to glory.

But that is not the end of the battle with darkness. In John 10:10, Jesus states: "The thief comes only to steal and kill and destroy; I have come that they may have life, and have it to the full." Once we choose salvation and welcome God's transforming work in us, we might be tempted to think that nothing can keep us from the full and abundant lives that Jesus desires for all of His followers. Unfortunately that is not always the case.

Every time that we, in our fallen human nature, make ungodly, sinful decisions, we open a spiritual gateway to the demonic realm. No Christian will walk through this life without sin, but when we turn to God and truly repent, we receive His gracious forgiveness. In most cases that is the end of it. Sometimes, however, we no longer commit certain sins after accepting the marvelous gift of salvation, but the activity we chose in the past still has an effect on our spiritual lives, as though it holds us in its grip. And then there are times that we seem to lose the struggle to break free from sins that entangle us: We continue to fall into the same snares; we continue to sin the same sins.

Because of sin we have aligned ourselves with Satan and his cohorts, better known as demons. More times than not the consequence of repeated sin is a demonic stronghold. In order to achieve breakthrough from these sinful choices and the resulting demonic grip, we have to be delivered and set free. This practice of being set free is called *deliverance ministry*.

I want to mention here that we will discuss the idea of Christians being demonized in greater depth in chapter 4, but let me stress for now that in order for this to happen there has to be an entry point for the demons. Demons know their legal rights; if the victim opens a door for them by sinning, they will make full use of their authority to inflict harm. The situation is further compounded because sometimes an individual suffers the consequences of sin committed by someone in his family line. Demonization can indeed result from sin in a previous generation—a curse that moves down the family line until it is dealt with. As Florynce R. Kennedy states: "There can be no really pervasive system of oppression . . . without the consent of the oppressed." And sometimes that consent was given years before.

A Quick Sketch of Deliverance Ministry

The American Heritage dictionary defines *deliverance* as "rescue from bondage or danger." *Bondage* is defined as "subjection to a force, power, or influence." Deliverance ministry, therefore, involves

- breaking demonic schemes and curses,
- casting out demons and
- releasing an individual from demonic oppression and influence.

As these bondages are broken, the captive is set free. Let's take just a brief look at each of these points.

Demonic Schemes and Curses

As stated above in John 10:10, the enemy comes to kill, steal and destroy. He will use any means possible to succeed in his battle against us, the children of God. These evil assignments can be an attempt to destroy a marriage, a destructive plot to extinguish a person's calling and ministry, a scheme to cruelly and prematurely end a life or a plan to rob all finances. This obviously is not an exhaustive list. The important point to understand is that demons execute evil schemes in the lives of their victims in order to produce bondage to hopelessness, death and destruction.

A *curse* is the practice of calling down evil or injury on someone or something. In deliverance ministry, curses are very common. The entry point of a curse can be obvious, such as in witchcraft when curses are purposely placed on or spoken against an individual. Curses can also be less obvious, like consistently repeated words of judgment. Examples of this are: "You are not worth anything"; "You will never amount to anything"; "You are fat"; "You are lazy"; "You are not wanted." When these words are spoken over a child by a parent, guardian or loved one, this child has been cursed.

Parents, listen to me: You cannot begin too early to protect your children from curses. When words of rejection are audibly spoken against an unwanted pregnancy or child in the womb, a door of rejection has been opened. We must guard our words as there is power in the tongue.

Casting Out Demons

The ministry of deliverance involves not only breaking evil power but casting out demons. We will discuss later how demons use the body of their victim to fulfill their evil desires. They take up residence in the person, attaching themselves to internal and external parts of the body. This is especially common in, but not limited to, occult activity, cult involvement, idolatry, sexual sin and a stronghold of bondage and infirmity. In these instances, manifestations include the movement of demons inside the body, which oftentimes can be felt and seen, or demons speaking through an individual. When this is the case, demons are commanded to "Get out!" in Jesus' name.

Demonic Oppression and Influence

Oppression means the cruel exercise of power over another. A person who is oppressed feels heavily weighed down in mind or body. You do not have to be involved in deliverance ministry for long to realize that this is the way demons treat their victims. They exercise their power callously, often hindering the mental and physical functioning of the captive.

Influence is slightly different. This is the power to affect something or someone. It is the ability to sway decisions or outcomes. Demons try to influence us to stand in agreement with sin and unrighteous activities. When we willfully accept this influence of evil, then authority has been released and an ungodly alliance has been established.

It is obvious that our choices affect not only our physical and mental well-being but our spiritual health as well. I was ministering recently to "Todd," a believer who had a major issue with alcohol abuse. (By the way, I have changed names and details throughout this book, including Todd's, in order to protect identities.) The pressures of life were weighing him down, and he was not able to go a day without consuming large quantities of alcohol. He was also suffering from a severe case of insomnia. Todd had not slept soundly for many weeks.

It was obvious to our ministry team that Todd was not looking to the Lord for help. He was numbing his pain and emotions through alcohol. He also had issues of unforgiveness, and Scripture is clear about how unforgiveness affects our spiritual freedom. Jesus told us: "For if you forgive men when they sin against you, your heavenly Father will also forgive you. But if you do not forgive men their sins, your Father will not forgive your sins" (Matthew 6:14–15). We do not have the luxury of holding on to unforgiveness; we are commanded to forgive. As we do so—and we will continue to discover this throughout our study—forgiveness achieves breakthrough from past wounds.

Our ministry team led Todd in a prayer of forgiveness toward those who had harmed him. He confessed his sins and repented of a bondage to alcohol. In Jesus' name we broke the power of and spiritual tie to that spirit of bondage. We announced to this demonic spirit that Todd's sleep would no longer be stolen, and that the assignment and allegiance made with a spirit of bondage no longer had a legal right to harass him.

This brother received complete freedom. He has not craved or touched a drop of alcohol since that time. His sleeping patterns were also healed; he now sleeps a full seven or eight hours every night. God is in the business of deliverance. He is faithful and truly desires to set free those who are bound by demonic oppression.

In sharing this story, I would like to make a point about semantics—and priorities. Was demonic oppression evident in Todd's life? Absolutely. Was demonic influence evident? Again, the answer is yes. But did it matter if we labeled the problem as such? Not really. In my experience in deliverance ministry, the most important thing to do is to focus on the issue at hand and deal with it scripturally. In other words, we did not waste valuable time or energy quibbling over how to label the problem. We knew there was a demon at the root of Todd's alcoholic bondage, and we desired passionately to break the grip of the enemy on our friend's life. This should always be the motivation and focus in the ministry of deliverance.

What about Demonic Possession?

Demonic possession is a term that confuses many people. *Possession* means, simply, being controlled. It is domination by evil spirits. In my experience in deliverance ministry, total possession is extremely rare. As we will see later in our exploration, a Christian can be *demonized*—that is, oppressed and influenced by demons—but I do not believe that a Christian can be *possessed* by demons. Nor can a non-Christian, unless he or she expresses the specific desire to be.

Several years ago I ministered to Hannah. This poor woman was unbearably tormented by demons and unable to function as a normal person. She threatened daily and many times attempted suicide. She was starving herself and never slept. Hannah's childhood was terrifying. She was raised in a home of Satan worshipers. I have never ministered to someone at such a desperate place. Her condition was literally life or death. This was the closest case I have witnessed to one of demonic possession. Even so, I am cautious about referring to such a stronghold of demonic activity as possession. Controlling *ownership* cannot be taken; it can only be given over by the victim.

As we began to minister, Hannah allowed the demons to take control over her whole being. She curled up in the corner of the room in a fetal position and spoke in a non-human voice. The team members and I commanded the spirits not to manifest their presence and to be quiet in Jesus' name, but the demons had a legal right to be there and were not budging.

The third time we met, I was able to achieve enough spiritual breakthrough in order to ask her if she had ever received Jesus as her Lord and Savior. She responded fearfully, "No. If I get saved, the demons have assured me that they will kill me." The team members began to enter into intense warfare intercession on her behalf. I presented the Gospel to her between the demonic manifestations of cursing and declaring that they were not leaving. I continued to press in and speak the truth of Jesus Christ's authority and the gift of salvation won for us at the cross.

I wish I could say that Hannah was saved that day, but she was not. Hannah was paralyzed with fear. Before leaving, we prayed over her asking the Lord for divine protection. We were deeply concerned about her safety and knew that without the Lord's defense and intervention, Hannah was in grave danger.

As she left, our hearts broke. We all continued to intercede and battle spiritually for Hannah. We were certain that this was her time of salvation. We refused to give up on her or to allow those demons to steal her life. A week later, I received a phone call. Hannah's friends had taken her to church where she prayed and received the gift of salvation!

From that point forward her life slowly began to change. The demons began to lose their hold, and she was able to experience freedom. It was a long process, but once the King of kings came into Hannah's heart she had the confidence to begin the battle of overcoming the demonic and to maintain the victories won. Jesus broke the power of the cruel domination of those evil spirits. Not even the strongest demons are able to possess the one who gives his or her life to Jesus.

Who Is the Deliverance Minister?

The deliverance minister is one who believes in Jesus and His blood-bought authority. It is in His name that the believer drives out demons and, by doing so, helps extend the Kingdom of God. This is Jesus' command in Scripture:

"And these signs will accompany those who believe: In my name they will drive out demons; they will speak in new tongues; they will pick up snakes with their hands; and when they drink deadly poison, it will not hurt them at all; they will place their hands on sick people, and they will get well."

Mark 16:17–18

All Christians carry authority over demons. While this is true, not everyone feels called to pursue a ministry of deliverance. Some know that this is their role in the Body of Christ; others respond to this challenge when necessary but are not involved on a regular basis.

Many deliverance ministers have a strong gift of discernment. This is the ability to differentiate between good and bad and also to see or hear in the spiritual realm. Revelatory gifts, such as prophecy, the word of knowledge and the word of wisdom, are also present in those called to this ministry. Some of the most powerful deliverance ministers I know operate with a strong gift of mercy.

I am often asked if the gift of discernment is a requirement for those involved in deliverance ministry. The truth is no. Doris Wagner of Global Harvest Ministries is an anointed deliverance minister. She answers this question in her book *How to Cast Out Demons* (Renew, 2000):

> Some of my friends have an unusually keen sense of discernment and can literally see demonic beings. They are usually correct, but I don't have a strong gift of discernment at all. However, my "gift of deduction" is rather advanced. Once you've been in the business any length of time, things fall into very predictable patterns and I am convinced that a great deal of the ministry of casting out of demons can be learned.

God is good to gift us according to our callings, and it is in our uniqueness that the Body of Christ is made whole. If you do not walk in discernment, you are by no means disqualified from deliverance ministry. You can learn what you need to know. It is my prayer that this book will help with just that kind of equipping.

Removing All Doubt

In closing this chapter, let me acknowledge the fact that not everyone believes in the validity of deliverance ministry. Many churches teach that the demonic realm does not even exist. In addition, cases of abuse by those who mismanage the tools of ministry have led to cries of malpractice; indeed, deaths have actually occurred among those seeking help and freedom. This is a grave issue.

In truth, the spiritual realm of good and evil is more real and alive than the physical realm in which we live. And because of the vast work of the enemy among us, we can no longer ignore the directive of Jesus to cast out demons and heal the sick. There are too many hurting and wounded children of God who need freedom. We are to be a victorious Bride. If, as the Church, we continue to ignore and disregard the issues in our lives that require deliverance and inner healing, the revival we so earnestly believe and pray for will not be fully realized.

Throughout this book, therefore, we will explore evidence of the demonic realm among us. Through testimonies and teaching we will view manifestations of evil—and study the scriptural call to combat them. We will learn effective practices to equip us, and we will highlight safeguards that will help us follow God's guidance and stay under His protective arm.

In short, deliverance ministry is vital to the Body. You and I can take part in this important work and help usher in the Kingdom of our wonderful Savior.

Our God is a good and faithful Father. Let's move ahead and begin our study by learning about the compassionate heart of Jesus our deliverer—and how He came to set people free.

2

Jesus the Deliverer

"The Spirit of the Lord is on me, because he has anointed me to preach good news to the poor. He has sent me to proclaim freedom for the prisoners and recovery of sight for the blind, to release the oppressed."

Luke 4:18

Put simply, Jesus came to preach salvation to humankind and to defeat the power of Satan. This is evident throughout His ministry: Jesus went about preaching the Good News that the Kingdom of God had come, and He demonstrated the power of that Kingdom by releasing those bound in darkness. Jesus said, "If I drive out demons by the Spirit of God, then the kingdom of God has come upon you" (Matthew 12:28). It is this supernatural supremacy that fills Satan and his minions with fear.

Jesus Sets the Example

As Jesus asserted His authority over Satan, the Kingdom of God was realized on earth. The New Testament is rich with these stories. Let's look at two examples.

Silencing an Unclean Spirit

Soon after beginning His earthly ministry, Jesus demonstrated that driving out evil spirits was a natural part of His mandate to set the oppressed free. This story is told in the gospel of Mark. It occurs after Jesus' baptism and temptation and after calling His first disciples.

> [Jesus and His disciples] went to Capernaum, and when the Sabbath came, Jesus went into the synagogue and began to teach. The people were amazed at his teaching, because he taught them as one who had authority, not as the teachers of the law. Just then a man in their synagogue who was possessed by an evil spirit cried out, "What do you want with us, Jesus of Nazareth? Have you come to destroy us? I know who you are—the Holy One of God!"
>
> "Be quiet!" said Jesus sternly. "Come out of him!" The evil spirit shook the man violently and came out of him with a shriek.
>
> The people were all so amazed that they asked each other, "What is this? A new teaching—and with authority! He even gives orders to evil spirits and they obey him."
>
> Mark 1:21–27

In Jesus' day, teaching in the synagogue usually meant expounding the Scriptures with much contemplation given to tradition and quotations from one rabbi or another. Jesus taught differently. The likely scene is that He was sitting and teaching out of His own wisdom and insight for an extended time while the amazed hearers simply listened.

The exact topic of this teaching is not given in Scrip. but it probably focused on His central message while on earth: The Kingdom of God has come near.

It was during His teaching that an evil spirit—unable to bear the true Word of God from the Son of Man—manifested itself. First, the demon, speaking through his human host, asked, "What have You to do with us? Have You come to destroy us?" This demon was not referring to itself and the man through whom it spoke; it was voicing concern over the threat that Jesus' presence and teaching posed for the demonic realm. In other words, this demon was issuing a challenge from the entire demonic army: "This is *our* kingdom, not Yours!"

The demon then acknowledged Jesus to be the Holy One of God. This might seem like a note of reverence, but it was not. The unclean spirit was attempting to gain control over our Lord by using His name and exposing His true identity. In ancient times names were considered to represent the very essence of an individual. To know a person's name—his or her essence—was to have power over that person. This confession was provoked by evil intent. This demon was trying to undermine the authority of the Savior.

Jesus understood the evil scheme behind this outburst and spoke immediately in the power of His authority. Most Bible translations interpret the rebuke as, *Be quiet!* Actually this is too nice. The modern irreverent phrase *Shut up!* is a more accurate translation of what Jesus said.

There are two aspects of this confrontation that I want to highlight briefly. First, notice that the defiant rebellious spirit left, but it did so with a shriek. Rest assured that if a demon made a final show of rebellion against the Lord in a deliverance setting, the same thing will occur when we issue commands in a deliverance setting.

Second, look at the events of Jesus' life at this point. Following Jesus' baptism, He was led by the Spirit into the wilderness for forty days to be tempted by Satan. Then

31

after standing successfully against His foe, Jesus began recruiting His disciples and teaching His message. It was not long before a demon confronted Jesus in another attempt to gain the upper hand.

Do you see the pattern? After Jesus' baptism and His Father's recognition of His calling and destiny, a spiritual confrontation between Satan and Jesus took place. Later, during Jesus' early days of ministry, a power confrontation between light and dark also occurred. We will see this pattern of God-directed activity followed by demonic attack throughout Jesus' life.

What does this mean for us? As we enter our God-ordained destinies, we can be sure that we, too, will face seasons when the schemes of darkness come against us and our ministries. Just as Jesus had to stand and overcome the temptations of Satan in the wilderness, we also will have times requiring a righteous stand. It is in these seasons that our blood-bought authority is tested and proven, and our faith and dependence on the Lord is stretched. This results in tremendous, transforming spiritual growth. We will learn throughout our study that it is by the authority of Jesus' mighty name, the power of His shed blood, standing on the authoritative Word of God, and a pure, devoted, focused heart that we overcome.

Healing a Demon-Possessed Man

Mark 5:1–20 tells the story of the man dominated by a multitude of demons called Legion. The traditional site of this supernatural deliverance is the eastern shore of the sea of Galilee, also called Gadara. Having just ministered in Capernaum, Jesus and His disciples crossed the sea where a violent storm almost overwhelmed their boat. Jesus responded in the power of the Creator and commanded the storm, "Quiet! Be still!" (Mark 4:39). As our Lord issued this decree, He was making known His authority in the region. The demonic realm was about to lose its hold.

Here is another instance of the pattern mentioned above. It is no coincidence that after exhibiting His divine authority over the storm, Jesus faced a power encounter with a demoniac. Jesus was, in fact, confronted by an assembly of demons that recognized Him and His spiritual dominance. Now is a good time to explain that following a supernatural event that gives honor to God and establishes Kingdom authority, the enemy will attempt to bring attention to himself while trying to intimidate the one through whom God is working. He does not like to lose ground.

> They went across the lake to the region of the Gerasenes. When Jesus got out of the boat, a man with an evil spirit came from the tombs to meet him. This man lived in the tombs, and no one could bind him any more, not even with a chain. For he had often been chained hand and foot, but he tore the chains apart and broke the irons on his feet. No one was strong enough to subdue him. Night and day among the tombs and in the hills he would cry out and cut himself with stones.
>
> Mark 5:1–5

This man was being controlled by demonic forces that were extremely violent. He was operating with inhuman, demonic, supernatural strength that chains and iron fetters could not contain. It was a common belief that demons lived in the tombs of the dead. Being drawn to darkness, this man lived naked and homeless among the dead bodies in the tombs. He would cry out continuously and cut himself with stones. This nameless man was in desperate need of freedom.

Mark 5:6–8 further explains:

> When he saw Jesus from a distance, he ran and fell on his knees in front of him. He shouted at the top of his voice, "What do you want with me, Jesus, Son of the Most High

God? Swear to God that you won't torture me!" For Jesus had said to him, "Come out of this man, you evil spirit!"

The Greek word used here for "bow" is *proskuneo*, which means to worship, to fall at one's feet, to bow low. The demons were not worshiping in the way you might think; they were actually pleading their cause. Jesus had just issued a command: "Jesus *had said* to him, 'Come out of this man, you evil spirit!'" (verse 8, emphasis added). The Lord had already delivered the eviction notice to these demons who understood His complete and absolute power over them. This is the cause of their bowing and begging and carrying on. They were pleading with Jesus because of their fear that He would pronounce the final judgment against them. Demons know when Christ-centered supernatural authority is present, and many times they will try to bargain or even beg to keep their victim bound. They want to continue their torment.

Then Jesus asked him, "What is your name?"
"My name is Legion," he replied, "for we are many." And he begged Jesus again and again not to send them out of the area.

Mark 5:9–10

Legion was actually a Roman military term referring to a unit of four to six thousand foot soldiers. Because of the strong Roman influence at this time, this term had become synonymous with "numerous" or "too many to count." The important point for our study is the fact that this man was being controlled by an enormous horde of demons. These demons not only succeeded in their unrelenting torment of this man, but they had also secured an influence in the region by gripping the Gadarenes with fear. They were acting as one in their torment and destruction of this man, as one in their assignment over the region and as one in their communication with Jesus.

In a desperate attempt to maintain their influence in Gadara, the demons then began to beg Jesus to send them into a herd of two thousand pigs that were feeding on the nearby hillside. He granted permission, and a legion of demons entered the pigs, which then rushed immediately into the lake and were drowned. Can you imagine the torment this poor man had suffered? The demons were powerful enough to destroy a herd of two thousand pigs.

The scene progresses in verses 14–17:

> Those tending the pigs ran off and reported this in the town and countryside, and the people went out to see what had happened. When they came to Jesus, they saw the man who had been possessed by the legion of demons, sitting there, dressed and in his right mind; and they were afraid. Those who had seen it told the people what had happened to the demon-possessed man—and told about the pigs as well. Then the people began to plead with Jesus to leave their region.

The Gadarenes wanted Jesus out of their country. Even though they had feared the demoniac, they knew what to expect from him. It was a case of poor management, but they felt they had the situation under control. But now a man more powerful than the demoniac was on the scene, and they had no clue how to deal with Him or His supernatural authority.

Does that sound familiar? The response of the townspeople resembles the fear and uncertainty of many in the Church today. They may preach a Gospel that reveals the power of the Son of God and His followers, but when they see the supernatural hand of God made manifest, especially in deliverance ministry, they are not sure that they want any part of it. Our God is an awesome God. His power to deliver should inspire worship and gratitude. We should long for the supernatural healing power of the King of kings, not resist it. Listen: I pray for the day that one command issued in the name of Jesus Christ will cause a legion of demons to flee.

In his enthusiasm and gratitude, the man begged Jesus to allow him to go with Him. Jesus answered with these words: "Go home to your family and tell them how much the Lord has done for you, and how he has had mercy on you" (verse 19). The man went to Decapolis and told all that had happened to him. Some translations state that he "published" all the Lord had done for him.

This man's testimony prepared the way for Jesus' future ministry in Decapolis, as noted in Mark 7:31–37. When the Lord arrived in Decapolis, He was greeted by a crowd of people asking Him to heal a man who was deaf and dumb. Deliverance ministry prepares the way for further supernatural moves of the Lord.

Jesus Calls Us to Follow Him

The Lord anoints and expects us as followers of His truth to exert power in His name over the demonic. Jesus' twelve disciples were the first ones to be appointed and commissioned with this authority to drive out demons.

> Jesus went up on a mountainside and called to him those he wanted, and they came to him. He appointed twelve—designating them apostles—that they might be with him and that he might send them out to preach and to have authority to drive out demons.
>
> Mark 3:13–15

The calling of the Twelve held a threefold purpose. First and foremost, they were to be with the Lord. As they spent time with Him, they would be transformed into His image and become like Him. Second, they were commissioned as apostles. *Apostelle*, the Greek word for "apostle," suggests a formal commissioning with the impartation of authority. The Hebrew word for "apostle" is *shaliach*, which indicates a representative. According to Bible commentaries, Jewish tradition held that a man's representative is as the man himself. These Twelve, therefore, were to preach the Gospel as representatives of Jesus Himself. Third, as representatives of Christ, the Twelve were to exercise authority over Satan and his cohorts. The ultimate purpose of the calling of the Twelve, of course, was extending the Kingdom of God. Remember that when the power of Jesus is exerted over darkness, the Kingdom of God is extended in the earth.

This calling to further the Kingdom did not stop, of course, with the Twelve. We read in Luke 10:17–19 that the Lord next commissioned 72 who would also confront the demonic.

> The seventy-two returned with joy and said, "Lord, even the demons submit to us in your name."
>
> He replied, "I saw Satan fall like lightning from heaven. I have given you authority to trample on snakes and scorpions and to overcome all the power of the enemy; nothing will harm you."

Upon their return, the 72 were amazed by the authority they exerted over demons. Jesus explained that they had the power to tread on darkness and to defeat the schemes of Satan and his demons. They had the authority to set people free from demonic oppression.

But Jesus wanted even more: He wanted to redeem the human race from sin and death and to destroy the power of evil itself. Jesus told His followers that He would accomplish this by His death on the cross:

> Now the judgment (crisis) of this world is coming on [sentence is now being passed on this world]. Now the ruler (evil genius, prince) of this world shall be cast out (expelled). And I, if and

when I am lifted up from the earth [on the cross], will draw
and attract all men [Gentiles as well as Jews] to Myself.

John 12:31–32, AMP

Other Scriptures also explain His purpose:

Since the children have flesh and blood, he too shared in their
humanity so that by his death he might destroy him who holds
the power of death—that is, the devil—and free those who all
their lives were held in slavery by their fear of death.

Hebrews 2:14–15

But now he has appeared once for all at the end of the ages
to do away with sin by the sacrifice of himself.

Hebrews 9:26

The reason the Son of God appeared was to destroy the
devil's work.

1 John 3:8

Jesus' early disciples learned to move in the power of His
name, and after His death and resurrection they stepped
out in new boldness to shine His light into the darkness.
The Good News is that the same blood-bought authority
is ours as followers of Jesus Christ. It is the power of our
Savior's blood that atones for the sin of humankind and
equips the Church for the ministry of setting people free.

As we move forward in this book, we will discuss our
authority over darkness in depth. In order for us to understand our role in the victory over darkness, we must first
understand our foe. Let's discover what the Bible teaches
about Satan and his demons.

3

WHAT DEMONS DO
AND WHY THEY DO IT

How art thou fallen from heaven, O Lucifer, son of the morning! how art thou cut down to the ground, which didst weaken the nations! For thou hast said in thine heart, I will ascend into heaven, I will exalt my throne above the stars of God: I will sit also upon the mount of the congregation, in the sides of the north: I will ascend above the heights of the clouds: I will be like the Most High. Yet thou shalt be brought down to hell, to the sides of the pit.

Isaiah 14:12–15, KJV

As we begin this chapter, I want to stress that as believers we have to be cautious not to focus too much on Satan and his demons. Do not, for instance, take the information in this chapter and begin to look for a demon behind every tree and around every corner. If our focus as Christians is on darkness, then the enemy has already won the battle, "for out of the overflow of the heart the mouth speaks" (Matthew 12:34). On the other hand, we have to be cautious against a spirit of passivity and underestimating the ranks of darkness "in order that Satan might not outwit us. For we are not unaware of his schemes" (2 Corinthians 2:11).

By learning about the traps of Satan and his minions, we can effectively stand against his lies and break his hold over our lives. The purpose of this chapter is to get us all "on the same page" concerning the purpose of the demonic realm in order to set people free.

Who Is the Enemy?

Lucifer, or "light bearer," is a name commonly ascribed to Satan. It is taken from the Latin translation of the Hebrew in Isaiah 14:12: "How you have fallen from heaven, O morning star, son of the dawn!" Lucifer was an archangel, a magnificent being, and was created by God, presumably, to hold high status in the worship of the Lord. Speaking prophetically, Ezekiel describes him as "the model of perfection, full of wisdom and perfect in beauty . . . anointed as a guardian cherub . . . on the holy mount of God" (Ezekiel 28:12, 14).

But Lucifer became full of pride, wanting to be like God. He apparently convinced a large company of angels to join him in rebelling against God, and their actions led to their banishment from the Lord's presence in heaven. Scripture refers to Lucifer after his fallen state as Satan or "adversary."

Satan's ultimate desires are to wage war against the Kingdom of God, to prevent true worship of our heavenly Father, to deceive humankind from the truth of the saving knowledge of Jesus Christ and to hinder the fulfillment of the Great Commission. He appears as an angel of light, the

40

counterfeit of the Son of God, thus deceiving and snaring those who believe his deception.

Here is a statement that we will hear several times throughout this book: Satan has never, nor will he ever, play fair! He is evil, deceptive, a liar, the destroyer, full of pride. There is nothing pure or good about Satan. God will bring this enemy to ruin and an eternity of torment by having him thrown into the fiery lake of sulfur in the final judgment:

> And the devil, who deceived them, was thrown into the lake of burning sulfur, where the beast and the false prophet had been thrown. They will be tormented day and night for ever and ever.
>
> Revelation 20:10

This outcome is fitting for Lucifer, the fallen morning star.

We learn a great deal about Satan and his attributes by the names used in reference to him throughout Scripture. He is devil, accuser of the brethren, tempter. He is the evil one, enemy, murderer, deceiver, Beelzebub, Belial—worthless one. He is the god of this age, prince of this world, prince of the power of the air, the great dragon, the ancient serpent, Abaddon and Apollyon—destroyer. He is the one who leads the whole world astray. He is the father of all lies.

What Satan Is Not!

Just writing the names of Satan causes righteous indignation to rise up within my spirit. As Christians, we view him as our foe. We should hate everything about him—all he resembles and embodies. I have great concern about a

41

teaching moving among Christian circles that suggests God wants to bring salvation and redemption to Satan and his army of darkness. This is false doctrine, a blasphemous lie. It causes the Church to grow sympathetic toward Satan, thus curbing our divine passion to war against his schemes on earth. The result is a deceived Church crippled by a tolerant, passive, apathetic spirit and mind-set toward the enemy of our souls.

Satan is not the evil brother of Jesus. He is a created angel who rebelled against our heavenly Father. He is not equal to God in any respect; he is not as equally evil as God is good. This is Luciferian doctrine that permeates secret societies such as Freemasonry and Eastern Star.

Satan is not omniscient, which means all-knowing. He is not omnipotent, meaning all-powerful. Nor is he omnipresent, which is defined as the ability to be everywhere at once. Only God is sovereign.

What Are Demons?

Satan has an army of demons to aid in his war against the Lord and the Body of Christ. The Greek word for "demon" is *daimonion*, also defined as "devil" or "evil spirit." There are several beliefs concerning the origin of these evil ones. Here are three prominent theories.

The first and most widely accepted view is that demons are fallen angels. As we noted above, when Satan rebelled against God he did not act alone. Revelation 12:3–4 tells us in its enigmatic language that the tail of an "enormous red dragon . . . swept a third of the stars out of the sky and flung them to the earth." This suggests that Satan had successfully influenced and enlisted one-third of heaven's angelic beings in his evil scheme. When the Lord cast Satan out of heaven, the same judgment was also given to the angelic hosts that joined in the rebellion. Gary Kinnaman explains this theory in his book *Angels: Dark and Light* (Servant Publications, 1994):

> The first theory, and the one I accept along with the great majority of Bible teachers, is that *demons are legions of fallen angels*. These are dysfunctional angels, serving the devil and making life miserable for human beings. There are several reasons for believing this view. First, there are parallel expressions like "the devil and his angels" (Matthew 25:41) and "Beelzebub, the prince of demons" (Matthew 12:24ff). It's obvious that the terms here are interchangeable, that the "devil" and "Beelzebub" are the same. So are "his angels" and "demons." I should point out, though, that Satan, who is a fallen angel, is never called a demon. Second, angels and demons seem to have the same nature. Both are called "spirits." Third, both demons and evil angels carry out the same terrible work, joining with Satan to oppose God and man.

Author and Bible scholar Derek Prince, in his discussions of the origins of demons, gives us the clearest view of the second theory. I do not profess to be a theologian, but after reading his fascinating and compelling reflections and having read other information I have researched on this subject, I am swayed to agree that this is also a very possible scenario. This is the idea that demons are disembodied spirits of a lost race on earth. His book *War in Heaven* (Chosen Books, 2003), which I highly recommend, offers this overview:

> Scholars have advanced numerous interpretations regarding the possible existence of a pre-Adamic race. Nonetheless Scripture does not provide us with sufficient evidence to speak with certainty. . . .
>
> However, I know of nothing in Scripture that implies that Adam was the first or the only being of a type similar to human who ever lived on the earth. I think it is entirely possible that there were one or more other races before

Adam, but the Bible does not deal with them. The Bible is primarily a revelation given to us as members of the Adamic race to tell us things that we need to know for our spiritual benefit.

In *They Shall Expel Demons* (Chosen Books, 1998), Prince points out several differences between demons and fallen angels:

> I must say . . . that on the basis of my experience, I find it hard to believe that demons are fallen angels. It seems clear to me that even fallen angels still maintain their dwelling place somewhere in "the heavenly places" (Ephesians 6:12)—although not "in the third heaven" where God dwells (2 Corinthians 12:2–4). It is not scriptural, therefore, to represent angels as operating continually on the plane of earth.
>
> Demons, on the other hand, appear to be earthbound creatures.
>
> Demons, as I have encountered them, display a wide range of character traits. Some are vicious, violent, supernaturally strong. Others are weak, cowering, even ridiculous—characteristics one would not expect to find in angels, even when they are fallen. . . .
>
> Let us suppose for a moment that [demons] are spirits that once occupied the bodies of members of some pre-Adamic race who led ungodly and sinful lives. In their present condition, however, they have no way to give expression to the various lusts and passions and emotions they developed in their former bodies. It is conceivable that they could find some kind of vicarious release by acting out their lusts or passions or emotions through human bodies. This would explain one dominant characteristic of demons: their intense craving to inhabit and work through human flesh. . . .
>
> It may be that neither of the two theories about demons is correct—that they are neither fallen angels nor disembodied spirits from an earlier race of beings. Our concept of demons, however, has a practical bearing on how we

deal with them. I have confronted many demons of different kinds, but have never had the impression that I was dealing with angelic beings.

On the other hand, I have had a certain amount of contact with satanic angels through intercessory prayer and spiritual warfare, which could best be described in the words of Paul in Ephesians 6:12: "For we do not wrestle against flesh and blood, but against . . . the rulers of the darkness of this age, against spiritual hosts of wickedness in heavenly places."

The New Testament does not depict Jesus or His apostles as "wrestling" with demons. Rather, they confronted demons . . . and exercised the authority needed to expel them.

A third hypothesis regarding the origin of demons is known as the Angelic Fall, which I believe to be the least likely of the theories. This belief stems from Jewish writings claiming that demons entered the world as a result of perverted sexual relations between angels and human beings. It is based on the interpretation of Genesis 6:1–2, 4, which says:

> When men began to increase in number on the earth and daughters were born to them, the sons of God saw that the daughters of men were beautiful, and they married any of them they chose. . . .
>
> The Nephilim were on the earth in those days—and also afterward—when the sons of God went to the daughters of men and had children by them.

The sons of God were believed to be angels who rebelled against God and procreated with the daughters of men. The outcome was the birth of the Nephilim who were said to be demons and evil spirits. In his book *Powers of Darkness* (Inter-Varsity Press, 1992), Clinton E. Arnold explains this theory:

> Many Jewish writers interpreted the reference to the "sons of God" as angels (called "Watchers"), who rebelled against

45

God. The disastrous consequence of this unnatural union resulted in the birth of the Nephilim, the source of demons and evil spirits. The Jewish apocalyptic book of 1 Enoch spends thirty-one chapters elaborating on this fall (1 Enoch 6–36). According to this account, after the physical beauty of women on earth erotically tantalized some 200 angels, led by a certain Semyaz, the angels made a joint decision to violate their divinely given boundaries by engaging in sexual activity with the women. While they were occupying the earth, they taught people many evil arts, including alchemy, astrology, incantations and warfare. The women made pregnant by these supernatural beings, gave birth to freakish giants. These giants committed numerous atrocities, yet their deaths did not prove to be the end of rampant evil—demons came from them:

"But now the giants who are born from the union of the spirits and the flesh shall be called evil spirits upon the earth and inside the earth. Evil spirits have come out of their bodies. . . . The spirits of the giants oppress each other; they will corrupt, fall, be excited, and fall upon the earth, and cause sorrow. They eat no food, nor become thirsty, nor find obstacles. And these spirits shall rise up against the children of the people and against the women, because they have proceeded forth from them."

1 Enoch 15:8–12

It was believed these evil spirits, which issued from the giants, would continue to corrupt humanity until the end of the age when God would put an end to their hostility and judge them. In Jewish literature this rebellion is referred to many times as responsible for the presence of demons. Meanwhile, the good angels, Raphael and Michael, have bound those angels who were guilty of this crime against women under the earth, where they will remain until the judgment.

1 Enoch 10:1–14 cf. Jude 6; 1 Peter 3:19–20; 2 Peter 2:4

Again, Scripture does not give us extensive teaching on the subject of the origin of demons. The important thing is for us to focus on the fact that demons are real and should be contended with in the authority of the name of Jesus Christ.

What Demons Do

The primary purpose of demons is to serve Satan in his conspiracy against God and His people. They are wicked and evil just like their master and commander. They will attempt every evil, vile, ungodly, reprobate act possible to perpetuate Satan's rebellion and prevent souls from coming into the Kingdom of God. The following are ways in which demons enforce the orders of their leader.

Demons Are Spirit Beings with Personalities

As we will discuss further in chapter 7, Scripture refers to demons by name. It becomes evident when dealing with demons in deliverance ministry that spirits of darkness have distinct personalities. A spirit of fear, for example, acts according to its label. In other words, the personality of the spirit of fear is fear. A spirit of death appears as death; it will try continually to place its captive in life-threatening situations. Here is an example involving these two spirits to give you an idea of how they work.

I was leading a team in ministry for a young man who was plagued with spirits of fear and death. The session was a powerful one as the Lord was moving on behalf of this man. As we progressed in prayer, the young man suddenly went limp in his chair. His entire body turned blue; he looked like a corpse. Needless to say, the team members fell silent, and then they looked at me with deep concern.

I have to admit this was a pretty intimidating demonic manifestation.

One of the team members whispered, "Is he dead?"

I shook my head and answered, "No."

I then began to break the power of a spirit of death from the young man and commanded it to go in Jesus' name. Once the command was given to that dark spirit, it left. The young man's skin color returned to pink.

He sat up in the chair and asked, "What happened? What did you do?" Before I could answer, he said joyously, "The demon is gone! Thank You, Lord!"

Demons Exploit Human Weakness

As humans, we are a fallen race. When we are weak and stumble into sin, we open the door for Satan and his demons to perpetuate evil—and they take full advantage of it. They work unceasingly to increase our tendency toward immorality and wickedness. As Paul told the Corinthians: "The sacrifices of pagans are offered to demons, not to God, and I do not want you to be participants with demons" (1 Corinthians 10:20). The willful, sinful practices of depravity can be considered as worship of evil and demons. Demons have and will continue to influence humankind toward any and every sinful behavior.

Demons Can Cause Illness and Torment

Demons can be the cause of illness. I am not saying all sicknesses are a deliverance issue, but many times demons or demonic generational curses of infirmity can be the source of disease. A scriptural example of a spirit of infirmity is found in Luke 13:11–13:

> And a woman was there who had been crippled by a spirit for eighteen years. She was bent over and could not

straighten up at all. When Jesus saw her, he called her forward and said to her, "Woman, you are set free from your infirmity." Then he put his hands on her, and immediately she straightened up and praised God.

Demonic spirits can also be a terrible source of torment in the life of an individual. This anguish can be so severe that it renders the captive helpless under the control of evil spirits and unable to function in a normal state. We already discussed the man with a legion in chapter 2. Another scriptural reference to this level of harassment and oppression is Mark 9:17–18, 22:

A man in the crowd answered, "Teacher, I brought you my son, who is possessed by a spirit that has robbed him of speech. Whenever it seizes him, it throws him to the ground. He foams at the mouth, gnashes his teeth and becomes rigid. I asked your disciples to drive out the spirit, but they could not." . . .
"It has often thrown him into fire or water to kill him."

Demons Mastermind Idolatry and False Religions

The masterminds behind all idolatry are demons. To worship an idol or pagan god is the same as bowing the knee to Satan and his demons. All pagan and idol worship stems from the demonic realm, clearly in opposition to the worship of Jesus Christ:

Jeshurun grew fat and kicked; filled with food, he became heavy and sleek. He abandoned the God who made him and rejected the Rock his Savior. They made him jealous with their foreign gods and angered him with their detestable idols. They sacrificed to demons, which are not God—gods they had not known, gods that recently appeared, gods your fathers did not fear.

Deuteronomy 32:15–17

49

False religions are also the work of Satan and his demons. All of the gods and goddesses worshiped in these religions have attributes similar to those of our Savior, but they are demonic counterfeits that deceive humankind, steal souls from heaven and extend the kingdom of darkness in the earth.

> Dear friends, do not believe every spirit, but test the spirits to see whether they are from God, because many false prophets have gone out into the world. This is how you can recognize the Spirit of God: Every spirit that acknowledges that Jesus Christ has come in the flesh is from God, but every spirit that does not acknowledge Jesus is not from God. This is the spirit of the antichrist, which you have heard is coming and even now is already in the world.
>
> 1 John 4:1–3

> The Spirit clearly says that in later times some will abandon the faith and follow deceiving spirits and things taught by demons.
>
> 1 Timothy 4:1

Demons Exert Influence over World Systems

In the past few years, the influence of demonic principalities, also known as territorial spirits, over world governments and religions has grown to a highly visible state. Demons are using those in power over nations and their beliefs in false religions to cause turmoil and death throughout the earth. The practice of dealing with these high-ranking evil spirits is termed strategic-level spiritual warfare. In my book *Authority to Tread*, I explain in depth how to pray at this level.

We find in the book of Daniel, in the prophet's vision of a powerful messenger, a strong scriptural example of the influence a territorial spirit can have over a government.

> "But the prince of the Persian kingdom resisted me twenty-one days. Then Michael, one of the chief princes, came to help me, because I was detained there with the king of Persia."

Daniel 10:13

The Persian prince in this reference was not human but was one of Satan's generals. It exerted power over the religions and the government of Babylon. These types of spirits are known as powers, principalities or territorial spirits. This demonic prince was so strong that Daniel had to wait 21 days for the heavenly visitor to break through with a particular revelation from heaven. Michael, also known as Israel's prince, was sent to wage war against this principality to make a way for the Lord's word to reach His prophet.

The following quote from Henry J. Hyde, chairman of the News Advisory Committee on International Relations of the U.S. House of Representatives (from a public e-mail dated October 26, 2005), is a modern-day example of a government that is influenced by demonic powers:

> Each year, thousands of North Koreans flee to China to escape a regime isolated by its dismal human rights record. What many refugees encounter in China, particularly women, is little better. Some fall prey to Chinese traffickers who force women into prostitution and abusive marriages, while others are forcibly returned to North Korea where they routinely face torture, imprisonment and sometimes execution. The government of North Korea also strictly curtails access to foreign broadcasts, considered a "crime against the revolution."

Demons Attach Themselves to Inanimate Objects

This is a scheme of the enemy used to gain entrance into our homes, businesses, schools, etc. Demons will attach themselves to items that lend themselves to darkness. Such articles can include books, music and artwork with a focus or emphasis on witchcraft, Satanism, false religions, idolatry and shamanism, just to name a few areas. They also attach themselves to icons and idols. When such objects make their way into our homes, demonic manifestations and harassment will follow. A great book to read on this subject is *Spiritual Housecleaning* (Regal, 2003) by Eddie and Alice Smith.

Demons Are Behind All Witchcraft and Occult Practices

Psychic power, tarot cards, palm reading, divination, Satanism, secret societies, witch covens, Wicca, astral projection, necromancy and yoga, with its roots in Eastern religions, are all works of the powers of darkness. All practices of witchcraft and the occult are birthed from Satan and his minions in order to deceive and bind humankind to their lies. Many involved in witchcraft and witch covens claim that they are not Satanists. While they might not be engaging in satanic rituals, their beliefs and practices are promoting the lies of Satan. They have indeed aligned themselves with darkness and are perpetuating wickedness and evil throughout the earth. They have become pawns of the enemy.

Scripture leaves no room for doubt concerning these demonic exploits. Here is one injunction among many:

> Let no one be found among you who sacrifices his son or daughter in the fire, who practices divination or sorcery, interprets omens, engages in witchcraft, or casts spells, or

who is a medium or spiritist or who consults the dead. Anyone who does these things is detestable to the LORD.

Deuteronomy 18:10–12

Demons Oppress and Influence Human Beings

The Bible is full of examples of how the enemy and demons inflict torment on men, women and children, and we have seen several modern-day examples in these first three chapters. In fact, I will close this chapter with the story of our family's first encounter with the reality of the demonic realm—when a demon began harassing our two-year-old daughter. Demons' sole purpose of existence is to serve Satan by waging war against the Kingdom of God and the Bride of Christ. They will use all means available to them to harass, torment, oppress and influence humankind. They delight in being evil and inflicting emotional, spiritual and physical confusion and anarchy into the lives of all people.

A Demonic Visitation

James 4:7 encourages us with these words: "Submit yourselves, then, to God. Resist the devil, and he will flee from you." My family first took these words to heart a number of years ago.

Our oldest daughter was always an easy child to care for. As an infant she slept through the night from the time she was five weeks old. One night, however, when she was about two years old, my husband and I were awakened from sleep at three in the morning by her screams. We rushed to her room to console her and could only get her calmed down by putting her in our bed. This happened again the following night.

The next morning I called one of our pastors to ask for help. I explained that we needed a prayer team to come to our home. Something in our house was scaring our child.

The pastor said, "You don't need a prayer team. Your daughter is seeing things in the spirit realm."

New to this concept, I gulped. "Seeing in the spirit realm?" I asked.

He told me that young children often see things in the spirit realm (angels and demons) and are typically taught that what they are seeing is not really there. It is explained away as just a bad dream or their imagination.

He gave us these instructions: The next time our daughter woke up afraid, we should go to her room and conduct a small interview. He said, first, to ask her "if she is seeing something." If she answers yes, we should then ask if what she is seeing is good or bad. If she answers good, she could be seeing an angel, and that can be scary to a small child. Even in Bible times angels scared folks! In that case we should explain that God has provided His angels to watch over and protect her while she sleeps; then lead her in prayer to thank God for His angels.

If she answers, "It's bad," we should demand quietly yet firmly in Jesus' name (in a manner that will not add to her fear) that it leave her room. Then pray and ask for God's angels of protection in the room.

That night it was difficult for Greg and me to fall asleep as we waited for her to wake up as she had the two previous nights. Like clockwork, at three A.M. she woke up crying and screaming. We jumped out of bed and nervously entered her room. Yes, we were a little apprehensive; after all, this was a first for us, too.

As soon as she saw us, she ran to us for comfort. We turned on the light and began to quiz her as our pastor had suggested. We asked, "Honey, are you seeing something?"

Nervously she answered, "Yes."

"Is it good or bad?"

"It's bad, Mommy. It's bad."

So we commanded the evil spirit to leave our daughter's room. We asked, "Is it gone?"

"Yes," she said. Then we asked the Lord to send His angels to watch over her. As soon as we finished praying, our daughter smiled and pointed with excitement, "Look, it's an angel! It's so pretty!" We then placed her back into her bed, and she quickly and peacefully drifted back to sleep. My husband and I left the room, awed at what we had witnessed and totally certain of the reality of demons.

The next night she again woke up screaming. We rushed to her room, but we were not as nervous this time. We asked her the same questions we had asked the night before, and her answers were the same. But as we prayed this time we led her to tell the spirit to leave her room in Jesus' name and to ask God to send His angels of protection. When our two-year-old daughter told the spirit to leave, the demon obeyed her. When she asked God for His angels, He sent them. Since then our daughter has remained sensitive to spiritual things and understands her authority in Jesus Christ.

Knowledge Builds Power for Action

Through this episode, my husband and I saw firsthand how the kingdom of darkness stands in blatant, blasphemous rebellion against the Kingdom of God. And this evil kingdom is very busy in its attempt to cause fear and destruction throughout the world. But we also got a powerful lesson in the authority of the believer. We came to realize that the more we understand the schemes of the adversary and his army of darkness, the more we are equipped as soldiers in the army of God to stand successfully against them.

The Good News is that the Kingdom of God will prevail, and all of darkness will suffer in an eternity of torment and torture. As stated in 1 John 4:4, "You, dear children, are from God and have overcome them, because the one who is in you is greater than the one who is in the world." The judgment has already been passed and sealed by the death, resurrection and ascension of our Savior, Jesus Christ.

Let's move forward, then, and learn how demons can influence the lives of Christians.

4

CAN A CHRISTIAN HAVE A DEMON?

May God himself, the God of peace, sanctify you through and through. May your whole spirit, soul and body be kept blameless at the coming of our Lord Jesus Christ.

1 Thessalonians 5:23

I have heard it said that a Christian can have anything that he or she wants. I have to agree! Having been involved in deliverance ministry for more than fifteen years, I have come to the realization that the Christian community struggles with problems—often overwhelming problems. And the majority of these problems seem to be rooted in thoughts and actions that—whether we realize it or not—invite demonic harassment.

Naturally no believer seeks trouble intentionally; and many an innocent person has faced the devil's wrath. But we have to admit that when spirits of fear, unbelief, rejection, heaviness, depression, passivity, generational curses, financial difficulties and marital strife continue to plague us, we are not walking in the victory that Jesus promised His followers.

This apparent contradiction leaves many Christians confused. On the one hand, we are called to be a victorious Bride who praises our God in spirit and in truth. Our lives are to be an example to the lost world so that those who do not have a personal relationship with Jesus Christ will be drawn to Him. On the other hand, believers too often choose ungodly behaviors, embrace sin and lead a life that does not model victory and freedom but one of victimization. The result is little or no distinction between the Christian community and the lost.

Since we are blood-bought children of the King, how can demons gain influence in our lives? Once we are saved, shouldn't the power of Jesus automatically negate demonic strongholds?

The fact is, the enemy is waging war against the Body of Christ. Christians have to learn how to shut the doors in our lives that are open to darkness. The responsibility and choice, ultimately, become ours.

Tripartite Beings

In order to understand the devil's access to our lives, we need to understand, first, the different "parts" of our makeup. The apostle Paul offers this insight: "May God himself, the God of peace, sanctify you through and through. May your whole spirit, soul and body be kept blameless at the coming of our Lord Jesus Christ" (1 Thessalonians 5:23).

The spirit, soul and body make up the whole or entire person. The Greek word for "complete" is *holothesis*. Dictionaries define this as "complete to the end, perfect, undamaged, whole through and through." To be found blameless at Jesus' coming, therefore, we must allow the Lord to work completely or through and through our entire being, which comprises these three separate entities.

Let's look at the creation of Adam to understand more fully the Lord's design for us as humans. This account, recorded in Genesis 2:7, reveals that this was a special act of God: "And the LORD God formed man of the dust of the ground, and breathed into his nostrils the breath of life; and man became a living soul" (KJV). Not only did God form man in His image and likeness, but the Lord imparted His breath and life into Adam, showing that human life stands in a category separate from other life, and that there is a connection between divine life and humankind.

Body

In creating Adam, the Lord first created a body: "The LORD God formed man of the dust of the ground." The human body, shaped and formed from the earth, has a special relation to the world; we might say that it is our world consciousness. The body has five senses—sight, sound, touch, smell and taste. It is a shell that houses the spirit and soul. Through it we live in and are a part of this world.

Spirit

God then "breathed into his nostrils the breath of life." This breath of life meant that Adam was no longer an empty shell but a man brought to life by the Spirit of God. The Hebrew word for "life" is *chaim*, which is plural in form and is interpreted as "lives." Derek Prince explains this in *War in Heaven*:

God breathed into Adam the breath of "lives." We find, as we go on throughout Scripture, that there are various forms of life: spiritual life and physical life, mortal life and immortal life. All these concepts are contained in seed form in this chapter of Genesis and developed in the subsequent unfolding of Scripture.

A similar process occurs when we receive the gift of salvation. When we are "born again," God breathes His life and Spirit into us. Our "spirit-man" is now alive and gives us God-consciousness. It is through the spirit that God speaks to us. As we worship, pray and spend time in the Word of God, our spirits are cultivated and grow. It is God's design that the body and soul walk in submission to the spirit.

Soul

The creation of Adam's body and the spirit that God breathed into him brought about this result: "And man became a living soul." The soul is composed of the mind, will and emotions; it allows self-consciousness. The soul was designed to walk in submission to the spirit so that we might follow God's will in all areas of our lives.

The Lord blessed Adam with a gifted mind; we see this foremost in his magnificent managerial skills. In short, God assigned Adam the task and ability to manage the earth:

> So God created man in his own image, in the image of God he created him; male and female he created them.
>
> God blessed them and said to them, "Be fruitful and increase in number; fill the earth and subdue it. Rule over the fish of the sea and the birds of the air and over every living creature that moves on the ground."
>
> Genesis 1:27–28

60

Can you imagine how powerful Adam was before the Fall? God gave him the capacity to rule and have dominion over all the earth, not to mention the aptitude for naming every living creature! Adam was a strong, brilliant, powerful man, hand-fashioned by God, but when he and Eve fell in the Garden, his soul power was hindered by the flesh. Watchman Nee gives a wonderful explanation of this in *The Latent Power of the Soul* (Christian Fellowship Publishers, 1972):

> According to Genesis 6, after the fall man becomes flesh. The flesh envelops the whole being and subjugates him. Man was originally a living soul; now, having fallen, he becomes flesh. His soul had been meant to submit to the spirit's control; now it is subject to the dominion of the flesh. Hence the Lord said, *"My spirit shall not strive with man forever, for that he also is flesh"* (Genesis 6:3). When God here mentioned man, He called him flesh, for in His eyes that was now what he was. Consequently it is recorded in the Bible that *"all flesh had corrupted their way upon the earth"* (Genesis 6:12); and again, *"upon the flesh of man shall it* (the holy anointing oil, representing in type the Holy Spirit) *not be poured"* (Exodus 30:32); and further, *"by the works of the law shall no flesh be justified in His sight"* (Romans 3:20).

Thank God that through Jesus' death and resurrection we now have access to salvation and the infilling of the Holy Spirit.

How Does This Apply to Us?

We are spirit, soul and body. God designed us so that the soul and body would be led by the spirit part of ourselves—the part that the enemy could not touch. Through Adam's disobedience, however, man entered spiritual death. Now Adam and his children would find that the willful soul would seek dominance in determining their thoughts and actions.

Jesus restored our broken relationship with the Father. Thus, when we are born again, things change. Our spirits are revived from death to life and can again enjoy intimate communion with the Lord. And since evil cannot reside in the presence of the Lord, our spirits are safe from the enemy's grasp.

Our souls are a different story. They remain open to the devil's attack—just as Adam's mind, not his spirit, was open to deception before the Fall. It is in our souls—our minds, wills and emotions—that the spirits of darkness harass, oppress and influence us.

This means that born-again Christians will be taunted and tempted to sin. If we resist the temptation, demons will have no right to attach themselves to our souls. If we fall into temptation, however, if we allow and embrace sinful thoughts and actions and lead an unrepentant life influenced by these rebellious choices, we have unlocked a door for the demonic in our lives.

Demons not only attach themselves to our souls but also use our bodies to operate through and fulfill their evil desires. Remember from chapter 3 that demons embrace the personalities of their namesakes. A spirit of perversion, for example, is perverse. This particular lustful demon needs a body to function through in order to fulfill its lustful desires. Another example is a spirit of bondage. This demon is responsible for all kinds of addictions. Whenever alcoholism, food disorders, pornography and drugs become addictive, a spirit of bondage has established a stronghold. It is through the individual that the demons experience the drugs, alcohol, pornography and any other addictions they long for.

Born-again Christians, therefore, can embrace sinful thoughts and practices that unlock a door for the demonic. When we give in to sin, we have become partners with the schemes of demons.

God gives all humans free will, or the right to make choices. Once we are saved, the power of choice is not taken from us. This means that even after conversion, we have the power or will to choose ungodly, evil practices. If we do, especially when it is a repeated sinful pattern, a door to darkness has been opened, permitting demonic activity in our lives.

The Power of Choice in My Life

I was saved at a Baptist youth revival when I was twelve. I will always remember the night I was baptized. As the preacher was lifting me up from the water, I felt a strong, wonderful presence of peace, love and acceptance descend on me. I did not know at the time what to call it, but I did realize it was a touch from the Lord. I now know it was the Holy Spirit resting on me. I was a new creature in Christ!

As I entered my teenage years, I read my Bible almost every night before going to bed and had a deep desire and hunger to know the Lord and the Word of God more. But like most teens, I faced peer pressure, and my desire to be accepted by the popular crowd was strong. I found myself slowly being drawn into the "party scene." Before long, I became a regular party attendee. My first two years of college, in fact, were mostly spent at all the hottest parties on campus. On the outside I was having fun, but on the inside I was miserable. I felt the conviction of the Lord almost constantly. But I had chosen a lifestyle of rebellion, and by doing so I permitted all kinds of ungodly influences in my life.

I was blessed to have family and friends who prayed for me. Actually, one of my best friends, whom I will call Amy, began to attend church and became very involved in the singles class. She put my name on the prayer list, and every Sunday that singles group prayed for me to get my life right with the Lord. Soon I felt a powerful pull of the Lord in my heart. I began to cry out for repentance, even in the midst of my sinful lifestyle. Upon returning home from party after party, I would lie in bed crying, asking the Lord for forgiveness, and read the Bible until I fell asleep. During this time, a powerful desire to meet a Christian man and to get married began to rise within me. Thank the Lord for praying parents, grandparents and friends!

After several months, Amy convinced me to attend church with her. It felt good to be with Christians and to worship the Lord again. In a short amount of time, I began going to all the church services and the singles functions. The party scene was slowly fading out of my life. I enjoyed my new friends from church. I particularly enjoyed getting to know one young man by the name of Greg. He and I started dating, but the enemy does not like to give up that easily. I was still riding the fence between two lifestyles.

Phone calls from my party friends were a daily occurrence. They would speak of how much they missed being with me and invite me to the next party. I declined many times, but they were persistent. Finally, I accepted an invitation. I thought it a great idea to go and share with them all the good things God was restoring in my life. Plus I just knew Greg would want to go with me and help me explain the changes I was making. This way I would not have to face everyone alone. I had a plan.

I arrived at Greg's apartment, confident that he would want to be a part of this noble cause. I will say right here and now, God knows whom to place us with. When Greg opened the apartment door, I shared excitedly where I was going and invited him to come along. He listened quietly to the invitation, but then responded abruptly, "I will not be a part of your rebellion. I will not go!" Then he slammed the door in my face! I am somewhat outspoken and feisty, and this made me mad. Now I was definitely going to the party to prove him wrong. He would see that I was no longer walking in rebellion. I would be able to go and withstand the temptation.

When I arrived at the party it did not take long before the games of peer pressure began. I had decided I would not drink that night, but my friends insisted. In an attempt to keep them quiet, I held a glass of beer in my hand with no intention of taking a drink. This worked for a few minutes, but they proceeded to measure the top of my glass to make sure I was drinking. The common encouragement repeated itself for quite awhile: "Come on, Becca. Take a drink! Come on, Becca. Take a drink!" So in an attempt to regain control of the situation, I decided to take a sip. As I did, something unexpected occurred: The beer tasted *awful*. For the past two years, it had been my drink of choice, but now the taste was nauseating. It even smelled terrible to me. This got my attention. What was happening?

Perplexed, I set the glass down and went to sit on the sofa. By this time, everyone was drunk and had forgotten about me. Suddenly all activity in the room grew still as I felt the Lord's presence beside me. I could not see Him, but I was aware that Jesus was standing next to me. I slowly and reverently turned toward Him. At this point, it was as if the room began to move in slow motion. The Lord started to point to every sin that was happening around me and said, *Becca, do you see that sin? That has been you for the past two years. Do you see that sin on the other side of the room? That has been you for the past two years.* He did this until every sin I had been involved in was pointed out to me. I was broken and humbled and knew I had to leave immediately.

Sobered by what had just transpired, I got up from that sofa, walked out of the apartment and headed for my car. As I walked, I was so overwhelmed by the reality of what I had become and the need to break out of this dark life that I said audibly, "Lord, I confess I have been in blatant rebellion and sin. Please forgive me and all I have stood for over the past two years of my life. I say no right now to this lifestyle, and I will never return. It is over and finished."

From that moment, I have never looked back. Nor have I had any desire to walk in that lifestyle again. As a believer, I had the power to choose a sinful life and I had the power to choose a righteous life. Because of the many wrong choices I had made, I had to go through a season of inner healing and deliverance. My rebellious and sinful choices had allowed demonic influences into my life that had to be dealt with and broken.

Deliverance Is for Believers

Deliverance is primarily for believers and not the lost. In order for a person to obtain complete liberty and a victorious life, he or she has to have access to the overcoming power of Jesus and the Holy Spirit. No one can continue the walk of freedom without the operating authority of Jesus. This is clearly stated in Jesus' words in Matthew 12:43–45:

"When an evil spirit comes out of a man, it goes through arid places seeking rest and does not find it. Then it says, 'I will return to the house I left.' When it arrives, it finds the house unoccupied, swept clean and put in order. Then it goes and takes with it seven other spirits more wicked than itself, and they go in and live there. And the final condition of that man is worse than the first."

After being cast out, the unclean spirit returns to its victim to find the filthiness of evil gone but the spiritual residence unoccupied. That evil spirit then brings seven other spirits to live in this "house." The latter condition of this man is far worse than the former. Even though this man was reformed and no longer embracing evil, his inward being remained unoccupied. Thus the door was open for demonic influence to return—and return as a much stronger force to be reckoned with. I will discuss this in more depth later, but I do not pray deliverance prayers over someone who is not intentional about receiving Christ.

My husband and I were small group leaders at a church we were attending. We encouraged our members to invite friends and loved ones to attend the weekly meetings. One night a young woman named Kim joined our group. She was shy and withdrawn, but she was also curious about the Lord. It quickly became obvious that Kim struggled greatly during times of worship. As soon as the presence of the Lord filled the room, she would have to leave. I prayed and asked the Lord why this was happening. He showed me that Kim was lost and in need of salvation. From that moment I began to intercede.

Kim continued to struggle in worship services in the home group, but during church services the battle was intense. She would sit on the back row of the church beside the aisle, and as the presence of the Holy Spirit flowed into the auditorium, she would bolt for the back door. Many loving and concerned members of the church prayed for her and commanded spirits of fear to leave in the name of Jesus. She was not able to keep the freedom. The torment actually grew worse as the spiritual battle intensified. I asked the Lord for permission to talk with Kim about her spiritual condition, but He clearly told me, *I am doing the work necessary to prepare her for salvation. She will come to you when the time is right.* I then understood that the Lord was personally bringing Kim to a place of desperation in order to receive the revelation of her lost condition. I aligned my prayers in agreement with the work of the Lord.

Several weeks later, a number of us were attending the annual women's conference at the church. In the early morning hours, the Lord woke me and told me that Kim would approach me that day asking me to lead her to the Lord. I was thrilled! As I entered the sanctuary where the conference was being held, Kim was waiting. She walked up to me quickly. "Becca," she said, "I know you have the answer to what is happening in my life. Will you please pray for me during the ministry time? Please set that time aside for me."

"Yes, I am here for you," I said, my heart full of joy. I was so excited about what was going to happen in Kim's life, I could not concentrate on the speaker's message.

As soon as the teaching ended, Kim and I situated ourselves in the back corner of the church. The Lord led me to read Romans 8:1–17. I could barely contain the tears as I read Paul's teaching on life in the Spirit versus life in sin. As Kim listened, I knew the Lord was revealing Himself to her.

When I had finished reading, she said, "Becca, God is telling me I am lost. I have prayed for salvation three times, and each time there was no fruit in my life. I prayed because I was told to and because I saw my other friends asking the Lord into their hearts, but with me it was never a heart issue. I have been trying to walk a Christian life without the gift of salvation." Her eternal salvation was secured that afternoon. Kim asked the Lord to forgive her for her sins, and she invited Him to be Lord of her life.

From that moment, Kim's life was on the journey of radical change. She was set free from a spirit of fear and rejection. She no longer fidgeted in the back row aisle seat at services; she made her way to the front and worshiped the Lord in total abandonment.

The Lord called Kim to missions, and she joined a church team on her first trip into another nation. God used her powerfully. She prayed for people who were marvelously healed and set free. The Lord also used her miraculously as an interpreter: Even though she could not speak the language, she was able to understand fully all that was being said to her. Our God is an awesome, saving, life-changing, delivering God!

Deliverance Is the Children's Bread

I find the Gentile woman in the story told in Mark 7:25–30 to be a shining example of the fact that freedom is obtainable and should be diligently sought after:

> In fact, as soon as she heard about him, a woman whose little daughter was possessed by an evil spirit came and fell at his feet. The woman was a Greek, born in Syrian Phoenicia. She begged Jesus to drive the demon out of her daughter.
> "First let the children eat all they want," he told her, "for it is not right to take the children's bread and toss it to their dogs."
> "Yes, Lord," she replied, "but even the dogs under the table eat the children's crumbs."
> Then he told her, "For such a reply, you may go; the demon has left your daughter."
> She went home and found her child lying on the bed, and the demon gone.

It is the responsibility of parents to do all that they can to help their children—especially true in desperate situations. This Greek woman threw herself at Jesus' feet, beseeching Him on behalf of her daughter who was possessed by an evil spirit. She was pleading for her child's freedom. In faith, she was placing herself and her daughter in the hands of the One who had the authority to help.

Jesus' response seems harsh and demeaning. But what did the Lord actually convey? That His ministry was first to the Jews and second to the Gentiles. He was not saying that the needs of the Gentiles would not be met, but that God's plan was for the house of Israel to receive the message of salvation first. I believe that Jesus was also trying to communicate that He was not abandoning His mission to the Jews, and if He granted this miracle, it would be an exception.

But why did He refer to her as a dog? In Scripture it is common for Gentiles to be called dogs. The term usually referred to ownerless scavengers roaming the streets. But as Jesus spoke to the woman, He referred to her as a little household pet that is valued and treated with affection and love. Pets that are loved have a place in the house of their owner. By expressing this sentiment, He was stating that even though she was a Gentile, there was a place for her and her daughter in the house of the Lord.

Responding in faith to the ray of hope in Jesus' answer, the woman explained that even household pets eat the crumbs that fall from the children's plates. In saying this, she expressed her understanding of the Lord's mission and graciously and confidently accepted the inferior position of a Gentile. She knew that Jesus was her daughter's only hope and diligently and humbly sought Him for the meager leftovers powerful enough to perform the miracle. She understood that she could be a partaker of the children's bread. Being moved by her sincere, faith-filled response, Jesus made the exception and set her daughter free.

We need to be inspired by this Gentile mother's refusal to accept her desperate condition. As Christians we no longer need to live in misery and defeat. Satan is the accuser of the brethren, and he is working above and beyond overtime to cripple the Body of Christ. If you are reading this book and feel discouraged, defeated, tormented or harassed by evil spirits, ask the Lord to set you free. If you have opened doors to the enemy, close them. Do not allow the lie that a Christian cannot have a demon to keep you from receiving the truth of the Lord and a life of freedom. Deliverance is truly the children's bread. God desires to set you free even more than you desire freedom. He is a good God!

5

CLOSING THE DOOR
ON THE ENEMY

"The thief comes only in order to steal and kill and destroy.
I came that they may have and enjoy life, and have it in
abundance (to the full, till it overflows)."

John 10:10, AMP

Scripture tells us that the enemy comes to kill, steal and
destroy. I will say it again: The enemy has never nor will he
ever play fair. He desires to use any means he can to blind
us from the truth, imprison us physically, emotionally and
spiritually, and hinder our destiny in the Lord. One of our
key defenses is to be aware of his schemes. Not only does
this knowledge provide protection against future attacks,
but it also helps us understand how to pray and break
established demonic influences in our lives. Several years

ago I attended a deliverance class taught by Doris Wagner, who shared this insightful quote from *The Perils of Passivity* (Frank D. Hammond, 2004), which clearly explains how the process starts:

> How do demons gain entrance into one's life? If demons could enter at will then each of us would be completely demonized. Demons cannot enter unless a way is provided for them. Gates through which demons enter can be identified. In fact, it is important that these gates be recognized as the prelude to deliverance and also that the gates can be successfully closed to prevent re-entrance of demons that have been expelled.

Let's discover, then, the doors the enemy walks through in order to establish strongholds in our lives.

Generational Curses

As we determined in the last chapter, the choices we make throughout our lives play a strong role in determining our spiritual condition. Choices we made in the past can continue to have a bearing on the present.

But we can look back even further: Sinful actions made by our ancestors in previous generations can actually open doors to demonic influences in our lives. The result is commonly referred to as a *generational curse* or *familial spirit*. (*Familial spirit* means "ancestral." As we will study later, the similar term *familiar spirit* refers to a spirit of witchcraft.) Until the sinful choices of ancestors are repented of and broken off the family line, future generations will continue to struggle with the same demons. This idea of passing down the effects of sin is found in the second Commandment:

> "You shall not make for yourself an idol in the form of anything in heaven above or on the earth beneath or in the

waters below. You shall not bow down to them or worship them; for I, the LORD your God, am a jealous God, punishing the children for the sin of the fathers to the third and fourth generation of those who hate me, but showing love to a thousand generations of those who love me and keep my commandments."

Exodus 20:4–6

When an individual struggles with an addiction to an abusive substance, for instance, more times than not past family members have endured the same bondage. It is not unusual to hear comments like this: "I suffer with an addiction to alcohol. My mother was an alcoholic, and her father was also an alcoholic." The enemy will keep a firm grip on the family line until the issue is repented of, all ties are broken and the demonic influence is cut off. Once I became involved in deliverance ministry, I learned quickly that generational curses are common, and almost any form of demonic oppression can be passed down from one generation to the next.

Willful Sin

Jesus said, "I tell you the truth, everyone who sins is a slave to sin" (John 8:34). Sinful practices and lifestyles that are embraced before and after salvation can and will compromise our spiritual position. We could describe *willful sin* as "deliberate action, use of the power of choice." As I found in my own experience of toying with sinful behavior, the consequences of willful sin have to be dealt with.

The following is not an exhaustive list, but it reviews the more common ways in which our will is seduced into ungodly behavior—and demons gain entrance.

73

Entertainment

The world of entertainment is flooded with blatant demonic connotations, images and schemes. Many movies, television shows, magazines, video games and books propagate the lies of darkness and establish demonic oppression in the lives of those who view them. Entertainment meant for children generally promotes witchcraft as a normal, everyday part of life and teaches the tenets of New Age and occult practices.

Scripture explains how this works. "Your eye is a lamp for your body. A pure eye lets sunshine into your soul. But an evil eye shuts out the light and plunges you into darkness" (Matthew 6:22–23, NLT). Thus, watching horror movies and television shows that focus on witchcraft and satanic practices is an entry point for a stronghold of witchcraft. Those that focus on sex and pornography can open the way to a stronghold of perversion and an addiction to pornography. Soap operas are filled with lust, lying and perversion, and if viewed on a regular basis become a source of lustful desires and an impure thought life. Observing ungodly activities in any form of entertainment presents the opportunity for darkness to flood our souls.

I am a professionally trained musician with a strong love for many genres of music. We play music in our home regularly. But I am keenly aware of the fact that the music industry is inundated with songs focused on sexual perversion, lying, drunkenness, etc. Many styles of music are purely satanic in nature and are meant to perpetuate the lies of Satan. I have heard the argument that the lyrics of songs and even satanic music cannot harm or influence those who listen to them. This is not true. Secular news media have reported how many teenagers, after attending rock concerts led by Satanists, returned home to commit suicide. Some teenagers who turn toward violence and murder state that the evil plots were planted in their minds by the satanic lyrics in songs. I have ministered to numerous individuals who suffered with a demonic stronghold because of the mode of music they listened to before and after salvation.

Games are another source of concern. Let me give you an example. One popular children's game that is quite dangerous is Pokèmon. I have ministered to children who have been plagued with violence, rage, nightmares, insomnia, allergies, asthma and other chronic illnesses due to their involvement with this game. Its origins are based in pagan worship, as John Paul Jackson shares in *Buying and Selling the Souls of Our Children* (Streams Publications, 2000):

> Pokèmon is rooted in Japanese culture and religious beliefs. Shinto as a belief system was incorporated into Japanese Buddhist practices beginning in the sixth century. Shinto is primarily a form of nature worship, where creative elements, such as earth, sun, water, rocks and trees are worshipped and personified. They believe these elements have a god behind their power. Interestingly, these features are also central elements portrayed in the game of Pokèmon.
>
> In Shinto, kami (spirits) are summoned through chanting and music. Chanting is a form of self-hypnosis and opens a demonic doorway to a person's soul. In Pokèmon, players are encouraged to chant the names of their Pocket Monsters. Some Pokèmon also chant or sing songs as a means to hypnotize or lull their victim to sleep.

My husband and I are the proud parents of three beautiful girls. We have both felt the crucial need to protect each of them from the snares of the enemy from the day they were born. We have especially taken the time to protect them from music, books, television shows and games that could trap them into the lies of darkness. From an early age, our girls have not been allowed to watch, read or listen to anything with overtones of witchcraft and perversion.

One afternoon, while they were still quite young, I was in the kitchen cooking dinner, and they were watching television. Our oldest daughter, Kendall, was the keeper of the remote while I was out of the room. I listened as they began to flip through the channels deciding what to watch.

"That looks like a good show," one of them said. "Let's watch it."

"Yeah, my friends really like that show," chimed in another.

Within a couple of minutes I heard Kendall exclaim, "We can't watch this! It has witchcraft in it!"

Her two little sisters readily agreed. "Hurry, Kendall!" they shouted. "Change the channel. This is bad!"

I smiled as I listened to my girls make a right and godly choice. As Scripture says, we are to train our children in the way they should go. And we are to be no less vigilant in our own choices.

If you are reading this book and have watched and listened to the types of entertainment that exalt sinful, ungodly activities, and you have never dealt with this, now is the time to do so. Confess your acceptance of these sinful activities and your involvement with them. Pray and ask the Lord to forgive you. Then audibly break all ties to the influence they have in your life in the name of Jesus. If you have movies, books, magazines and music in your home that are evil and demonic, throw them away or burn them. Remember from chapter 3 that demons attach themselves to inanimate objects.

Substance Abuse and Other Addictions

Addictions can take many forms—drugs, alcohol, nicotine, gluttony, eating disorders, overspending, gambling. I like Noel and Phyl Gibson's definition of addiction from *Evicting Demonic Intruders* (New Wine Press, 1993):

"When choice is replaced with compulsion, a person is an addict."

The reasons for addiction often fall into three general categories: because of deep pain or trauma, because of an emotional void or because a need is not being met. Many addicts are lonely, hurt, disappointed, grief stricken, angry and oftentimes struggling with unforgiveness.

Let's take a closer look at drug and alcohol abuse. Experimentation with drugs almost always leads to addiction. The habit of taking drugs for mind-altering purposes originates in ancient witchcraft practices. The Greek word for "drug," in fact, is *pharmakon*. This word is derived from the Greek word *pharmakeuein*, which is defined in Webster's dictionary as "the practice of witchcraft." This is also the root of our words *pharmacy* and *pharmaceutical*. Witchcraft is the originating, primary force behind drug use and addiction. If you tampered with drugs in the past, it is crucial for you to confess that past participation, repent and break the spirits of bondage and witchcraft.

Alcohol abuse is also a formidable trap of the enemy. I am not saying that drinking alcohol is a sin; each individual has to hear from the Lord concerning his or her consumption of alcohol. But we must remember Paul's warning about drunkenness: "Do not get drunk on wine, which leads to debauchery. Instead, be filled with the Spirit" (Ephesians 5:18). Drunkenness and debauchery were actually the goals in some pagan religions. In ceremonies honoring Bacchus, also known as the wine god, worshipers would get heavily drunk, abandon all inhibitions and perform acts of perversion. This is obviously an extreme example, but any abuse of alcohol is dangerous and potentially deadly.

It can prove a tremendous battle to break the firm grip gained by a drug or alcohol addiction. A demon of bondage has to be addressed and the physical body cleansed.

Sexual Immorality

The Bible tells us that the marriage bed is to be undefiled. Why is the Lord so clear about this in Scripture? It is because the act of sex is not only a physical union but also a spiritual union. This union is meant to unite one man and one woman, consummating the covenant made before God in a marriage ceremony. The Lord designed sexual intimacy to be holy, pure and treasured. It is in the secret and sacred place of the marriage bed that the part of ourselves created to be pure and set apart is given away and a spiritual and emotional tie is created.

Sadly, the defilement of the marriage bed has become commonplace in our society. Sexual sins such as promiscuity, fornication, adultery, homosexuality, pornography, lust, bestiality and other immoral acts have been embraced as an accepted part of culture. When these rebellious acts of sexual perversion are participated in, powerful doors to the demonic realm are opened, and a spiritual and emotional connection known as a *soul tie* is formed between the individuals involved.

Soul ties are formed between those who jointly engage in sinful, ungodly practices. They are also established in acts of violation and trauma and in relationships based on ungodly control and unhealthy emotional attachments. Once a soul tie is established between two individuals, the demonic can transfer from one person to the other. In other words, if one of the participants struggles with a spirit of pride, this demon now has access to the other person. The result is double trouble.

I prayed for a young woman who had been sexually involved with a boyfriend in high school. She was happily married with children, but nightly was plagued with dreams of her high school sweetheart. And during the day her thoughts were bombarded with images of him, their sexual activity and perverse and lustful desires. She had not shared with her husband the torment she was experiencing, but even so it was beginning to affect their relationship. She had repented of her sexual involvement with this boy and had rebuked the recurring dreams, but to no avail; they continued.

I asked, "Have you broken the ungodly soul tie between the two of you?"

She thought for a moment and replied, "No, I have not. Can you please pray and break the hold this has on me? I desperately want these dreams and thoughts to stop. I love my husband, but I feel unfaithful and guilty."

We prayed and broke the power of the ungodly tie of perversion, whoredom and lust that was still operating between the two of them and commanded all demonic influences that were released in her life as a result of this sexual relationship to leave. Shame and guilt are greatly prevalent in those who have lived an immoral lifestyle. We commanded these spirits to go in Jesus' name. Instantly she felt something lift off her shoulders and mind, and she began to receive further revelation. She suddenly remembered that she had saved all the cards and love notes from this boyfriend. They were stored in a box in her attic. She quickly went home and destroyed them all. To this day she is totally free.

Rebellion

Scripture compares rebellion to the sin of divination: "For rebellion is like the sin of divination, and arrogance like the evil of idolatry" (1 Samuel 15:23). *Divination* is seeking to control people, events and even the future by the departed spirits of the dead. Because rebellion is ultimately manipulation, it is a form of witchcraft.

I believe the first step toward rebellion is lying. Once several lies have been told without consequence, a lying spirit has been embraced, and the pattern is set. Those involved in rebellion do not listen to authority figures, nor do they seek the Lord for His purposes in their lives. They remove themselves from God's protection and, thereby, open doors to all forms of physical, emotional and spiritual danger.

Unforgiveness

The willingness to forgive is vital to a life of freedom and victory. Jesus said this: "If you forgive men when they sin against you, your heavenly Father will also forgive you. But if you do not forgive men their sins, your Father will not forgive your sins" (Matthew 6:14–15). Christians must be ready and willing to forgive the offenses of others. If we do not forgive, then our heavenly Father will not forgive our sins. This means that we are not to wait for an apology from the offender, nor do we keep a running checklist of wrongs directed at us.

The choice to forgive is done before any offense has developed and without any expectation of an apology or repayment. Forgiveness is a lifestyle choice. We make the decision to walk in forgiveness even before any breach of trust, hurt, betrayal or violation has occurred.

When Peter came to Jesus asking how many times a brother should be forgiven, Jesus responded with the parable of the unmerciful servant.

> "Therefore, the kingdom of heaven is like a king who wanted to settle accounts with his servants. As he began the settlement, a man who owed him ten thousand talents was brought to him. Since he was not able to pay, the master ordered that he and his wife and his children and all that he had be sold to repay the debt.
>
> "The servant fell on his knees before him. 'Be patient with me,' he begged, 'and I will pay back everything.' The

80

servant's master took pity on him, canceled the debt and let him go.

"But when that servant went out, he found one of his fellow servants who owed him a hundred denarii. He grabbed him and began to choke him. 'Pay back what you owe me!' he demanded.

"His fellow servant fell to his knees and begged him, 'Be patient with me, and I will pay you back.'

"But he refused. Instead, he went off and had the man thrown into prison until he could pay the debt. When the other servants saw what had happened, they were greatly distressed and went and told their master everything that had happened.

"Then the master called the servant in. 'You wicked servant,' he said, 'I canceled all that debt of yours because you begged me to. Shouldn't you have had mercy on your fellow servant just as I had on you?' In anger his master turned him over to the jailers to be tortured, until he should pay back all he owed.

"This is how my heavenly Father will treat each of you unless you forgive your brother from your heart."

Matthew 18:23–35

A sobering truth in this Scripture is the obvious anger of the Lord toward those who do not forgive. If we hold grudges, expect repayment and embrace unforgiveness toward another, the Lord says plainly that He will turn us over to be tortured. This is not something I want to experience in my life!

Think about this. As Jesus hung on the cross, He cried out, "Father, forgive them, for they do not know what they are doing" (Luke 23:34). Jesus did not wait for an apology from those who were taking His life. He cried out for mercy and forgiveness. Jesus' death on the cross establishes redemption for all who will come to Him, even those who have hurt, betrayed or sinned against us. Christ paid for their sins once and for all just as He did ours. As His followers, we should mirror His example.

81

Our heavenly Father is loving, merciful and gracious toward all of His children. We have done nothing that is deserving of this love. Even so, He faithfully extends forgiveness, releasing each of us from our debt of sin, and He expects us in return to be merciful and gracious to those who have sinned against us.

Forgiving Ourselves

This idea of forgiveness extends to the way we treat ourselves. Many times it becomes evident in deliverance ministry that people have made terrible choices and hurt others because of demonic oppression. Usually these individuals feel guilty and have a hard time forgiving and releasing themselves from their actions of the past. Even though God has forgiven them, they continue to beat themselves up and are unable to move forward.

We have all been involved in terrible mistakes leading to pain and loss. Even though the unpleasant events cannot be erased, life-changing lessons can be learned from the poor choices and can prove to be a great blessing. The truth is that Jesus died on the cross to forgive our sins. Our trespasses are swept clean because of His great sacrifice. If we then choose not to forgive ourselves, we have in essence said that the sacrifice Jesus paid was not enough.

Failing to Forgive

Unforgiveness is dangerous mentally, emotionally, physically and spiritually. Tormenting thoughts, strained relationships, physical illness and barriers in our relationship with the Lord can all come from focusing on the wrongs done to us and refusing to release them. We may think that we are somehow "getting even" by harboring bitterness and unforgiveness, but we are actually causing distress and bondage to ourselves.

I have not heard a better teacher on forgiveness than Eddie Smith. In *Breaking the Enemy's Grip* (Bethany House, 2004), he explains the consequences of refusing to forgive:

> When we refuse to forgive, God deals with us on four levels.
> - Conviction. Initially, God convicts us. Guilt is a powerful motivation for us to confess, repent, and return to Christ. If we fail to respond to His conviction, He will chasten us.
> - Chastening. When chastening us, God uses circumstances to get our attention. This could include sudden unemployment, financial difficulty, unexpected expenses, or many other factors. Hebrews 12:8 (CEV) says, "God corrects all of his children, and if he doesn't correct you, then you don't really belong to him."
> - Scourging. When the Lord is forced to scourge us, we're in serious trouble. Scourging is what Jesus referred to in His story of the king and the debtor; scourging is when God releases us to the tormentors. For instance, Paul warned the Corinthian believers about taking the Lord's Supper (Communion) with sin in their hearts: "Examine your motives, test your heart, come to this meal in holy awe. If you give no thought (or worse, don't care) about the broken body of the Master when you eat and drink, you're running the risk of serious consequences. That's why so many of you even now are listless and sick, and others have gone to an early grave" (1 Corinthians 11:28–30, MESSAGE).
> - The Sin Unto Death. If we overlook God's conviction, chastening, and scourging, we literally run the risk of committing the sin unto death. This is the last thing the Lord wants to do, but if we proudly and arrogantly insist and persist, we leave Him no choice.

Walking in Forgiveness

Many years ago, I witnessed an unrighteous and unjust situation suffered by someone I love. It did not take long for me to harbor thoughts of unforgiveness and bitterness toward the individuals who had betrayed my friend. After several days, I realized in my prayer time that there was a wall between myself and the Lord. I began to search my heart and discovered the unforgiveness. I confessed, repented and released all the hurt, pain and betrayal to Him. I asked the Lord to help me love with His love the individuals who had so angered me.

He was faithful to answer this prayer; my heart was supernaturally flooded with love and compassion for those ones. To this day, when I am in the presence of these fellow Christians, my heart is full of compassion, and I truly enjoy our time together. Bitterness did not take root in my heart.

I now understand the power of blessing those who persecute us. When hurtful situations develop, our response is critical. Choosing to forgive produces the character of Christ. By extending forgiveness, we are released from the hurt and pain. In these trying times we can develop great spiritual growth and dependence on God.

Brothers and sisters, this is crucial to understand. Even when we are falsely accused, forgiveness and humility break the back of the enemy. Reaching out in the love of our Savior will initiate healing and restoration. I have learned in my Christian walk that the Lord is able to fight my battles far more successfully than I am. He is in the business of restoration. If God is for us, who can be against us?

The Occult

Any participation in occult activity is a red carpet invitation for demons. The occult entices those hungry for the supernatural and draws them into a web of deceit and destruction. What exactly is the occult? James S. Wallace explains in *The Occult Trap* (Wagner Publications, 2004):

Occult is a term that refers to a wide range of practices, beliefs, and phenomena, which are beyond the realm of empirical, scientific knowledge. There are three distinct characteristics of the occult: (1) it deals with things hidden or secret, (2) it deals with operations or events which seem to depend on human powers that go beyond the five senses, and (3) it deals with the supernatural, the presence of angelic or demonic forces.

Almost all practices and objects associated with the occult can be classified under one of three main categories: (1) divination, (2) magic, or (3) spiritism. All of these forms of the occult are interrelated and there is some overlap between them. The occult is a primary instrument of Satan to deceive people and turn them away from God.

Occult activities include all practices associated with witchcraft and satanic worship. The following is a list of beliefs and practices that fall under occult activity. A more extensive list is included in the appendix.

Astrology

Chakras

Channeling

Clairvoyance

Divination

Eastern religions

ESP

Fortune-telling

Freemasonry and all forms of this secret society

Horoscopes

Idolatry

Karma

Magic

Mantras

Martial arts

Mind-altering drugs
Necromancy
New Age meditation
Ouija boards
Palm reading
Psychic power
Satanism
Séances
Spirit guides
Tarot cards
Telepathy
Water witching
Wicca
Witchcraft
Yoga

I will not take the time to discuss each of these top-ics because that would take another whole book. Two great resources to add to your library that have extensive information and lists on the occult are *Deliver Us from Evil* by Cindy Jacobs (Regal, 2001) and *The Occult Trap* by James S. Wallace, mentioned above. I do, however, want to discuss three of these topics briefly, because believers usually take part in them without fully understanding the demonic connections. These three are martial arts, yoga and Freemasonry.

Martial Arts

As I travel and teach about deliverance ministry, I find that some people resist the idea that the martial arts grew out of Buddhism and Taoism. Still, it is true. There is a pagan religious heritage at the core of these fighting sports. The *Dictionary of Cults, Sects, Religions, and the Occult* by

George Mather and Larry Nichols (Zondervan, 1993) gives this insight:

> The religious significance of the arts lies in the harmonizing of life forces (Yin and Yang) and the ability to harness "Ch'i" [universal energy]. Masters in the martial arts accomplish tremendous physical feats. The ability to strike or kick with tremendous physical force or to smash a pile of bricks with a single blow is attributed to "Ch'i."

Martial arts such as aikido, judo, jujitsu, karate, kung fu, ninjitsu, ta'i chi ch'uan and tae kwon do have pagan and ungodly roots and open doors to the demonic. I have witnessed those who have dealt with intense spirits of anger and violence because of participation in martial arts. If we open ourselves to something with demonic pagan roots, even if it is done unknowingly and innocently, demons still have access to our souls.

I have heard the argument that God can make the martial arts pure, meaning that Christians can participate in an abridged form of the activity without fear of demonic connection. I do not believe that God is concerned with making the martial arts pure. If something started as a demonic, pagan religion or practice, then it remains a demonic, pagan religion or practice. Our Father is not in the business of remaking an evil ritual that Satan designed. He desires to destroy the works of Satan in our lives and throughout the world. The Lord tells us in Scripture that we are to keep ourselves pure and holy. We are to be separate and consecrated from the practices of the world and the enemy.

Yoga

The word *yoga*, meaning "to yoke," comes from the Sanskrit language. Yoga is a Hindu system of philosophy. Here is Webster's definition:

> A mystic and ascetic discipline by which one seeks to achieve liberation of the self and union with the supreme spirit or universal soul through intense concentration, deep meditation, and practices involving prescribed postures and controlled breathing.

The whole system of these exercises is derived from the worship of Eastern deities. Countless Christians attend and even teach yoga classes without fully comprehending that they are opening their souls up to spirits of error, Antichrist and witchcraft.

I find it ironic that as believers we will spend money on organic vegetables, water purifiers and all-natural products in order to protect our physical bodies from pollutants and toxins. We will go to great lengths to show our displeasure when local stores place immoral publications on their shelves. But then we follow a yoga instructor, opening our souls to demonic deities that will affect not only our spiritual lives but those of future generations. Our spiritual condition should be a priority. We need to know what doors we are opening into our souls.

Freemasonry

I deal with Freemasonry on a consistent basis in deliverance ministry. Large numbers of men and women have been members or have a family history of participation in this secret society. On the surface, Freemasonry appears as a reputable organization. Membership involves, for instance, generous contributions to reputable charitable organizations, and many important historical figures have been members. But just as we discussed concerning martial arts and yoga, Freemasonry also has pagan, demonic roots.

Freemasonry has its origins in the worship of Isis, Osiris and Horus, pagan gods of ancient Egypt, and all the tenets of this secret society come from the worship of these demons. The following is a quote from *Morals and Dogmas* (L. H. Jenkins, Inc., 1950), a book written for Masons that explains the origins behind the Rituals of Degrees. The author is Albert Pike, who was the Grand Commander of the Scottish Rite for the Southern Jurisdiction of the United States from 1858 to 1891. It discusses the 25th Degree, Knight of the Brazen Serpent.

> This Degree is both philosophical and moral. While it teaches the necessity of reformation as well as repentance, as a means of obtaining mercy and forgiveness, it is also devoted to an explanation of the symbols of Masonry; and especially to those which are connected with that ancient and universal legend, of which that of Khir-Om Abi is but a variation; that legend which, representing a murder or a death, and a restoration to life, by a drama in which figure Osiris, Isis and Horus, Atys and Cybele, Adonis and Venus, the Cabiri, Dionusos, and many another representative of the active and passive Powers of Nature, taught the Initiates in the Mysteries that the rule of Evil and Darkness is but temporary, and that that of Light and Good will be eternal.

Freemasonry endorses the Luciferian doctrine, which, as I mentioned earlier, declares that Satan is just as evil as God is good—meaning that the enemy is as powerful as our heavenly Father. It teaches that men become gods. All members are free to worship the deity of their choice and are told that the god they worship is the true way to eternal life. Unfortunately, many of these beliefs are not revealed until a member has reached the higher levels of leadership in the Lodge.

The list can go on and on concerning the anti-Christian foundation of Freemasonry. After reading the little bit of information above, we can see how easy it is for membership in the Lodge to release a curse on the member and his family. A spirit of death and infirmity are common spiritual conditions of members. It is not unusual for sudden, premature and unexpected deaths of active members to occur. A spirit of witchcraft, an Antichrist spirit, a lying spirit and a spirit of Mammon are very prevalent in those who have actively participated in or have a family connection to Freemasonry.

I have prayed for numerous individuals who were steeped in the occult before salvation. When pacts and covenants have been made with spirits of darkness, even after salvation the torment can prove to be intense. Demons do not like to give up their hold on those who have so readily embraced their supernatural force. But greater is He who is in us, than he who is in the world! Our God is an all-powerful, faithful, delivering God.

Open Doors of Trauma

Even though we may have no choice in events that traumatize us, they still give Satan an open door. Remember he does not play fair and will take advantage of an unsettling experience to gain a foothold. Webster's defines *trauma* as "a bodily injury, wound or shock; or a painful emotional experience or shock that often produces a lasting psychic effect."

Such an event might include but not be limited to the following:

Rape
A violent attack
Car wreck
Traumatic accident resulting in an injury
Rejection in the mother's womb
Parents driven by rage and anger
Excessive teasing by schoolchildren or family members

Being picked on or beaten up by a childhood bully

Alcoholic parents

Sexual abuse

Molestation

Death of a loved one

Long-term period of unemployment

Pornographic material seen as a child

Being violated or victimized by another person

Desertion or divorce

Unfair treatment by a teacher or authority figure

Total disappointment or being let down by trusted individuals

It is in this time of pain and emotional distress that the enemy will fill the one violated with thoughts of fear, confusion, anger, rejection, bitterness and unforgiveness. As these emotions take hold, the victim becomes bound by the tormenting event.

Betty had been struggling with fear for many years. She was afraid of authority figures and also felt she would be abandoned by those who loved her. She was convinced that she would die at a premature age. Desperate to receive freedom, she contacted me.

It was not long into the ministry time that the Lord revealed a sad picture of her childhood. I asked her, "Betty, what was your father like?"

She paused for a moment as her eyes filled with tears. "He was an alcoholic. He was always depressed and very seldom kept his word to me or my brothers and sisters."

Feeling a strong impression that there was more to find out, I continued, "Was there a certain promise he made to you, but broke?"

Barely even able to speak in a whisper, she replied, "Yes. It was my sixth birthday. He promised he would arrive home on time to take me and my friends to a pizza parlor for a birthday party. I was elated. I loved my dad and wanted badly to have a loving father-daughter relationship with him. I stood at the living room window waiting eagerly for him, but he never returned that night. After work, he went out drinking with his friends and totally forgot about me and my party. I was crushed. He never even acknowledged that he had forgotten it. A year later, he died unexpectedly in our home. I was the one who discovered his body."

What a sad, terrible, traumatic lifestyle for such a young girl. During these events, trauma gripped Betty's mind, will and emotions. Her life was tormented by fear, abandonment and the fear of death.

In her young mind, the enemy began to plant lies. Her thought life was filled with accusations such as, *All those who love you and all those you love are going to leave you. You'd better not allow anyone to get too close. No one cares about you. Remember how your dad died; the same is going to happen to you.* The enemy took advantage of her young age and lack of understanding and established a foothold.

Betty struggled with her issues until the day we prayed for her. Sometimes the effects of a severe trauma do not appear until later in life. The good news is Betty forgave her father and received healing in her mind, will and emotions. The spirits of fear, abandonment and fear of death were commanded in the name of Jesus to leave. She is now walking in total freedom. She is happily married and enjoys many friends.

Sadly, when traumas take place in the form of violence such as rape, child abuse and sexual molestation, ungodly soul ties are established, keeping the victim bound to the attacker. It is difficult, but even in these circumstances the injured party must forgive the assailant. As stated above, forgiveness is a command of God and a choice that has to be made. When we walk in obedience and choose to forgive even when our emotions dictate not to, the effects of the traumatic event are lifted from our lives. Forgiveness is an act of obedience to the Word of God; our emotions will catch up in time.

It is important to understand that forgiveness and trust are not the same. Forgiveness can happen in an instant; it usually takes time for trust to be regained in a relationship. This is normal. But please note that in the case of perpetration, forgiveness does not mean friendship or even contact. Never allow a chance for another violent attack.

Moving On

The enemy is our foe, and he has many ways in which he works against the children of God. And we have to admit that we have the power and prerogative to choose ungodly lifestyles. When sin rules our lives—whether from occult activity, unforgiveness, addictions or some other action that grieves the Holy Spirit—we must seek the forgiveness of our Savior and close any doors that we have opened. If trauma has given the enemy an opportunity to be exploitive, then we must realize that Jesus Christ is our Lord and that the Holy Spirit is able to meet our needs and to cleanse and heal our pains.

We are blood-bought children of Jesus Christ with God-given authority to deal with every scheme of the devil. Let's move ahead and learn more about who we are and the authority we carry.

6

AUTHORITY OF THE BELIEVER

Behold, I give unto you power to tread on serpents and
scorpions, and over all the power of the enemy: and nothing shall by any means hurt you.

Luke 10:19, KJV

We have authority in the name of Jesus! Authority means
that we have the right to give commands. We can make
the final decision in spiritual conflict with evil, and we
can enforce obedience. I have heard people say from time
to time that they do not want to participate in deliverance
ministry or spiritual warfare because they do not want to
have any altercations with spirits of darkness. The truth is,
once saved, we have enlisted in the most powerful army
in the universe: the Bride of Christ. In this army there is no
way to avoid contact with the enemy. But we do not have
to fear. The authority bestowed on us as children of God

comes from the blood of Jesus. And He said to all of His followers, "I give unto you power."

Scripture equips us with plenty of strategies for using that authority in battle. For our purposes of deliverance ministry, I want to focus on three biblical guidelines in these next three sections. When we grasp these concepts, we will find it much easier to move in our rightful authority and help set people free.

Exercising Legal Authority

Because we are members of the army of God, we have the legal right to exert power over the enemy in the name of Jesus. And we have territorial rights, too. Put generally, legal power usually involves a certain jurisdiction, and jurisdiction implies the ability to administer justice in a particular area.

What area? The apostle Paul gives us the answer and the basis for our first guideline: "We are therefore Christ's ambassadors, as though God were making his appeal through us" (2 Corinthians 5:20). We are ambassadors—the personal representation—of the heavenly Kingdom to the earthly kingdom. This means that we have Christ's authority throughout the whole realm of earth! God works directly through us to combat the works of evil and darkness and to spread the glorious message of the Gospel of Christ.

Does this sound amazing? There is more.

I assure you, most solemnly I tell you, if anyone steadfastly believes in Me, he will himself be able to do the things that I do; and he will do even greater things than these, because I go to the Father.

John 14:12, AMP

Consider this for a moment: Jesus desires for us to do *greater* works than He did. When He ascended to the right hand of the Father, Jesus left us with the directive to extend the Kingdom of God by performing supernatural works. True disciples of Christ draw lost men, women and children to salvation, walk in authority over darkness, heal the sick, teach the Word, cast out demons. We show that the Gospel of Christ is genuine and it is in His name and power that the miraculous is performed.

Jesus described some of these miraculous acts to His disciples:

> And these attesting signs will accompany those who believe: in My name they will drive out demons; they will speak in new languages; they will pick up serpents; and [even] if they drink anything deadly, it will not hurt them; they will lay their hands on the sick, and they will get well.
>
> Mark 16:17–18, AMP

These signs and miracles were not intended to end with the ministry of Jesus or that of the twelve apostles. They are to continue until the Savior returns. These gifts are available to all who are followers of Christ. When miracles do not occur in the Church, it is not because our Lord has failed to keep His promises; rather it is because we have chosen not to walk in the power given to us as His disciples. When we do, however, we learn what His earliest followers learned: We can minister as true God-ordained ambassadors in the earth.

Those early followers were amazed by this authority. We read in Scripture that after commissioning the twelve disciples, Jesus sent out 72 of His followers to spread the Kingdom message.

The seventy-two returned with joy and said, "Lord, even the demons submit to us in your name."

He replied, "I saw Satan fall like lightning from heaven. I have given you authority to trample on snakes and scorpions and to overcome all the power of the enemy; nothing will harm you."

Luke 10:17–19

These followers found that demons were forced against their will to submit to the authority of Jesus Christ. Demons know that a believer acting as Jesus' ambassador has legal authority in spiritual matters, and they know they must submit. The Greek word for "submit" actually denotes involuntary submission or obedience out of fear. After years of ministering to those held in bondage, I can attest personally to the fact that demons shudder with fear at the name of Jesus.

Just as the 72 trampled over darkness in Jesus' name, so we are called to help advance the army of God. Jesus expects us to move forward in our positions as His ambassadors and take the Good News to the ends of the earth.

The Key Ingredient

Jesus is the deliverer and we are His representatives, walking in blood-bought authority to cast out demons. If this takes some getting used to, remember that even the disciples did not understand this privilege at first. Scripture tells of their failed attempts involving a boy who needed deliverance. In their experience we find our second guideline: Walking in authority means walking in faith.

When they came to the crowd, a man approached Jesus and knelt before him. "Lord, have mercy on my son," he said. "He has seizures and is suffering greatly. He often falls into the fire or into the water. I brought him to your disciples, but they could not heal him."

Matthew 17:14–16

It is generally believed that this young boy was suffering from symptoms of epilepsy that were demonically induced. Scripture tells us that he was besieged and tormented by a deaf and dumb spirit—and the disciples could not cast it out.

Jesus' dismay over His disciples' failure to exercise their authority is evident:

> "O unbelieving and perverse generation," Jesus replied, "how long shall I stay with you? How long shall I put up with you? Bring the boy here to me." Jesus rebuked the demon, and it came out of the boy, and he was healed from that moment.

Matthew 17:17–18

Jesus expected His disciples to walk in the power of His Kingdom. Not to do so was deemed as faithless and crooked in the eyes of our Lord. He cast out the demon, and from that very moment the boy was healed.

Maybe this was the disciples' first unsuccessful attempt in dealing with a demon; maybe they were surprised by their ineffectiveness. They asked Jesus to explain why the demon remained in spite of their attempts at deliverance:

> Then the disciples came to Jesus in private and asked, "Why couldn't we drive it out?"
>
> He replied, "Because you have so little faith. I tell you the truth, if you have faith as small as a mustard seed, you can say to this mountain, 'Move from here to there' and it will move. Nothing will be impossible for you."

Matthew 17:19–20

99

Their problem was lack of faith, unbelief. Unbelief is tantamount to distrust. The disciples were followers of Christ, but by not possessing the faith necessary to cast out the demon, they were exhibiting the mind-set, lack of understanding and disbelief of unbelievers.

The reference to a mustard seed points not only to size but also to quality. Just as a tiny mustard seed is planted in the ground and grows into a serviceable tree, so faith in Christ can be cultivated and grow in usefulness. Time spent in worship, in the Word and in the presence of the Lord will result in increased faith. This faith, by the way, is placed in God and not in the gift of faith itself. As we partner with God we will see the release of Kingdom power—and the demonized will be set free.

As we have seen, the disciples had to learn how faith affects ministry, and most of us are no different—I certainly was not. Let me show you what I mean.

When I first began praying with Alice Smith and the deliverance ministry team of our church on a regular basis, I thoroughly enjoyed seeing the demonically oppressed set free. But I was in the school of deliverance and about to have my own lack of faith revealed.

One day we were scheduled to pray for a woman whom we had ministered to on several occasions. God was moving powerfully in her life, but she still had strong issues to address before walking in complete freedom. When I got out of bed that particular morning, I felt a strong, enveloping presence of the Lord. I was not certain why I was experiencing this, but I was fairly sure it had something to do with the upcoming ministry.

As I was about to leave the house, the phone rang. It was Alice. She explained that she had an unexpected conflict and would arrive late for the ministry appointment.

She then said, "Becca, I want you to lead the team until I arrive."

I replied nervously, "Alice, I am so new to this. The other team members have been praying longer with you and are more experienced. You should ask one of them."

"You are the one I am asking," she said. "You will be fine."

As we hung up the phone, I whispered a fervent prayer: "Lord, please help me with this ministry session. I do not know what I am doing. I cannot do this without You."

Everyone arrived on time for the scheduled ministry appointment, including the woman who was in need of prayer. To be honest, I was so nervous that I had secretly hoped she would not show up. That was not the case.

As we began to pray, it did not take long for the demons to show themselves. I did not express it on the outside, but on the inside I was completely intimidated. I did everything I could think of. I spoke every prayer I could remember from prior sessions with the ministry team. I rebuked the demons in the name of Jesus. I quoted Scripture. I asked the Lord to send His warring angels. Nothing happened. Those demons were not budging.

About this time, Alice entered the room. She sat quietly in the back of the room, watching as we ministered. Now my personal struggle greatly intensified. Not only did I not have authority over those demons, but Alice was seeing my incompetence. Thoughts of failure, insecurity and self-pity raced through my mind. I knew I would never be asked back to another deliverance session.

After observing for a few minutes, Alice approached the woman and rebuked the demon, and it left instantly. I sat down in a chair and watched her complete the ministry time. I thought to myself, *Becca, you have no authority and no business ministering deliverance.*

As the session ended and the team left, I was making my way down the hallway, totally discouraged. Alice called my name. I will never forget the words she spoke to me. "Becca," she said, "remember, the demons are 'learning' you just as you are 'learning' them. The more you grow in the Lord and pray in the authority the Lord has given you, the more they will learn who you are and tremble."

I broke into tears and thanked her for the encouragement. From that day forward, I started to grow in authority in deliverance ministry and have never again allowed a lack of faith to interfere when dealing with demons.

What to Guard Against

So we need to understand first our position as ambassadors and then the essential role of faith as we pray for those who are in need. What is our third guideline for walking in authority? We must guard against presumption. The seven sons of Sceva teach us this lesson well:

> Then some of the traveling Jewish exorcists (men who adjure evil spirits) also undertook to call the name of the Lord Jesus over those who had evil spirits, saying, I solemnly implore and charge you by the Jesus Whom Paul preaches! Seven sons of a certain Jewish chief priest named Sceva were doing this. But [one] evil spirit retorted, Jesus I know, and Paul I know about, but who are you? Then the man in whom the evil spirit dwelt leaped upon them, mastering two of them, and was so violent against them that they dashed out of that house [in fear], stripped naked and wounded.
>
> Acts 19:13–16, AMP

The authority Paul demonstrated gained the attention of seven itinerant Jewish exorcists. These men traveled throughout the area claiming to have power over demons and after charging a fee would use magical formulas to deal with them. There is no record in the Bible that their ministry was successful.

102

Then one day they observed the power operating through Paul when he spoke the words "in the name of Jesus." They came to the conclusion that Paul was employing a magical formula and decided to try it themselves. They used the name of Jesus as a charm to make money. Obviously, the sons of Sceva had not embraced the message of salvation through Jesus Christ. They missed entirely the fact that Paul was being obedient to the call on his life to preach the true word of God. They did not understand that the Lord was using the signs and wonders to confirm Paul's life-changing message. These men were presuming a great deal and heading down a dangerous path.

When they tried to cast out a demon using the name of Jesus as a magic charm, one demon spoke up: "Jesus I know, and Paul I know about, but who are you?" (This is not exactly what you want to hear as a deliverance minister!) Presumptuously, the seven sons took upon themselves an authority that was not rightfully theirs. These demons recognized and acknowledged the power of Jesus operating through Paul, and they were certain it was not functioning through the sons of Sceva.

Having now the advantage, the demons took full control of the situation. Using the body of the man they inhabited, those demons leaped upon the sons of Sceva, overpowering them. It is important to say right here that demons can and do use the bodies of their captives. The strength that was exerted through this man was supernatural and inhuman in force. The attack was so effective that the sons of Sceva fled the house naked and wounded. The Greek words used in this passage indicate that the wounds were severe enough to last for a while. This was an all-out assault.

The point of this story is not to invoke fear or turn anyone away from deliverance ministry, but to help keep things in the right perspective. Deliverance ministry is not a vehicle for flexing our spiritual muscles or showing off. I should also mention that deliverance ministry is not the place for someone who is struggling with problems and hoping to get helped by helping others. A deliverance minister who is bound, for instance, by a stronghold of lust and pornography must never try to help deliver someone who is struggling with those same issues. More times than not in this setting the two demons gain strength from each other, increasing their hold. And there is a strong possibility that the demons in the deliverance minister will foster altercations and counterattacks with the person seeking healing in order to inhibit his or her freedom. No one who is involved in pornography, adultery, fornication, unforgiveness, addictions, witchcraft or any other ungodly activity should ever be actively praying in deliverance ministry. It is dangerous and will achieve nothing positive.

Our goal is quite different: ministry under the anointing of the Holy Spirit and the power of Jesus to help set people free from demonic oppression. When we set aside presumption and follow the Lord's guidance, we have nothing to worry about. Let me share an experience where Jesus' authority and protection far surpassed a demon's outburst of rage.

Our ministry team had gathered late one afternoon to minister to Sarah, a young girl who was in an intense spiritual battle and in desperate need of freedom. The ministry session began and was running smoothly. The Lord revealed to me that Sarah had root issues of child sexual abuse by a family member. I brought this into the open.

"Sarah," I asked, "were you sexually abused as a child?"

"Yes," she said through tears.

"We would like to pray about that. This will be a key issue to deal with in order for you to receive freedom. You will need to forgive the man who did this to you. Are you able to do this?"

She nodded, obediently forgave the responsible family member and released him to the Lord. The team then began to deal with the demonic spirits that were operating in her life. She was gaining great freedom.

We began making the final blows to the strongholds attached to this traumatic event. "In the name of Jesus," I said, "I break the power of all perversion, whoredom and child sexual abuse off of—"

Before I could finish my sentence, a scream came out of Sarah, and her body was catapulted out of her chair. She seemed to be coming through the air at me, shouting in an inhuman voice, "I am going to kill you!" Her hands were extended toward my throat.

All of this happened a lot more quickly than I can tell it. I did not have time to think clearly how to respond. The Lord took over. Under the anointing of the Holy Spirit, I stood to meet her, and as she got directly in front of my face with hands extended, it was as if she hit an invisible wall. The force of the impact threw her backward in the air and onto the floor. She had not touched me. Instantly the team members and I dropped beside her on the floor and commanded the spirit to leave in Jesus' name. It obeyed, but left with an ear-piercing shriek.

Sarah sat up and exclaimed, "I am so sorry! I do not know what came over me, but whatever it was, it is gone now!"

This all happened in a matter of seconds, but when God is in control, the outcome is victorious. When we desire to move under His leading and leave presumption behind, He provides the shield of protection for those ministering deliverance.

Are You Ready?

We have learned about the authority we have to move as Christ's ambassadors, to grow in faith and to flee from presumption. In addition we must always remember that our spiritual condition is important if we are engaging in deliverance ministry. No one wants to have a "seven sons of Sceva" experience! Scripture teaches us:

> But as the One Who called you is holy, you yourselves also be holy in all your conduct and manner of living. For it is written, You shall be holy, for I am holy.
>
> 1 Peter 1:15–16, AMP

We can no longer live lives controlled by sin; we are called to obedience and holiness. It is probably safe to say that none of us will obtain perfection on this side of eternity, but I do believe we can reach levels of holiness where we experience extended periods of time without sin. If we ask the Lord, He will help us. He will show us how to move in His authority. He will be faithful to answer this request.

Are you ready? Let's learn more about the authority that comes from being able to identify demons by name.

7

DIAGNOSING DEMONS

The wise in heart are called discerning, and pleasant words promote instruction.

Proverbs 16:21

Any soldier will tell you the importance of knowing your enemy. Few things can provide better advantage in battle. The same principle applies to deliverance ministry. Being able to identify demonic beings and to call them by their names—particularly the names revealed in Scripture—wields powerful and effective authority. This is one of the most common subjects during the question and answer sessions of my deliverance seminars and the subject we will address here: How do we know what demon to deal with? What are the names of demons? How do we know if something is really demonic as opposed to fallen human nature?

The Gift of Discernment

Let's start with perhaps the key ingredient in diagnosing demons: the spiritual gift of discernment. Paul lists this as one of the manifestation gifts:

> Now to each one the manifestation of the Spirit is given for the common good. To one there is given through the Spirit the message of wisdom, to another the message of knowledge by means of the same Spirit, to another faith by the same Spirit, to another gifts of healing by that one Spirit, to another miraculous powers, to another prophecy, to another distinguishing between spirits, to another speaking in different kinds of tongues, and to still another the interpretation of tongues. All these are the work of one and the same Spirit, and he gives them to each one, just as he determines.
>
> 1 Corinthians 12:7–11

Discernment means basically the ability to differentiate between good and bad. In the passage above it is used to describe one of the gifts of the Holy Spirit—ways He enables believers to operate with supernatural power. In this regard, discernment refers to spiritual insight allowing one to distinguish between good and evil and, further, to determine the origin of spiritual activity. In *Discover Your Spiritual Gifts* (Regal Books, 2002), Peter Wagner states: "Discerning of spirits is defined as the special ability to know with assurance whether certain behaviors purported to be of God are in reality divine, human or satanic."

Suppose we discern that a certain behavior is satanic; do we always discover the name of the demon to be dealt with? The answer is no. But we can learn to decipher demonic patterns and behaviors and come close. Demons are not very creative. It took only a few months in active deliverance ministry for me to begin to learn their patterns of deception. Many of them are very similar.

We will examine a few of the more common names and categories of demons in a moment. First, however, I want to address this question: How do we know if someone's negative behavior is a demonic manifestation as opposed to human nature and sinfulness? The two can sometimes look alike. Here is an example from Scripture that helps us understand the difference.

Human Nature versus Demonic Manifestation

Many times what might appear as demonic is really human nature and fleshly desire at work. Desires stem from our emotions. When our emotions are not aligned with the thoughts and plans of God, we can make decisions that ensnare us or cause us to stumble—even when our intentions are good, as the apostle Peter found out.

> From that time forth Jesus began [clearly] to show His disciples that He must go to Jerusalem and suffer many things at the hands of the elders and the high priests and scribes, and be killed, and on the third day be raised from death. Then Peter took Him aside to speak to Him privately and began to reprove and charge Him sharply, saying, God forbid, Lord! This must never happen to You! But Jesus turned away from Peter and said to him, Get behind Me, Satan! You are in My way [an offense and a hindrance and a snare to Me]; for you are minding what partakes not of the nature and quality of God, but of men.
>
> Matthew 16:21–23, AMP

Jesus knew He had to prepare the disciples for His death. As the Messiah spoke, I can imagine Peter's reaction. It was probably one of shock, disbelief, love and deep concern for the Son of God: "This must never happen to You!" He was not acting out of evil intent but out of the thoughts and emotions of a man. As one of my reference books, *Complete Biblical Library*, observes, Peter, who was earlier called the "rock," had now become the stumbling stone (World Library Press, 1991).

Jesus corrected Peter in the same manner as when He was dealing directly with Satan. But was an evil spirit operating through Peter? No. Peter's reaction was driven by the flesh; he was acting out of an earthly, humanistic way of thinking. He did not have the mind of God on this matter and, as a result, set a snare for Jesus. We cannot fathom the inner battle that Jesus was already experiencing with the knowledge of torture and torment in His very near future. The last thing He needed was someone He loved telling Him that His crucifixion and resurrection were not the will of God. The cross was a divine plan, and Peter's human nature—well-meaning though it was—stood in direct opposition to the Lord's destiny of bringing redemption to humankind.

This example from Scripture shows us how choices and decisions made "in the flesh" can look like demonic influence. They can be just as effective at setting up traps and stumbling blocks in our lives—and others' lives. We also see how discernment in ministry is vital in order to distinguish the issues of human nature from those of the demonic. We cannot cast out our human nature, but we can repent and get back on track by once again falling into line with the will of our Father.

Recognizing Demonic Spirits

Let's turn now to another scriptural account that helps us learn to discern and diagnose demonic spirits in operation. Here is the account of Ananias and Sapphira—and the numerous demons that we can identify based on their story:

> Now a man named Ananias, together with his wife Sapphira, also [like Barnabas] sold a piece of property. With his wife's full knowledge he kept back part of the money for himself, but brought the rest and put it at the apostles' feet.
>
> Then Peter said, "Ananias, how is it that Satan has so filled your heart that you have lied to the Holy Spirit and have kept for yourself some of the money you received for the land? Didn't it belong to you before it was sold? And after it was sold, wasn't the money at your disposal? What made you think of doing such a thing? You have not lied to men but to God."
>
> When Ananias heard this, he fell down and died. And great fear seized all who heard what had happened. Then the young men came forward, wrapped up his body, and carried him out and buried him.
>
> About three hours later his wife came in, not knowing what had happened. Peter asked her, "Tell me, is this the price you and Ananias got for the land?"
>
> "Yes," she said, "that is the price."
>
> Peter said to her, "How could you agree to test the Spirit of the Lord? Look! The feet of the men who buried your husband are at the door, and they will carry you out also."
>
> At that moment she fell down at his feet and died.
>
> Acts 5:1–10

Imagine! I think we all will agree that it is obviously not a wise idea to lie to and grieve the Holy Spirit. The Lord did not allow this sin to go unnoticed.

Peter was operating in strong and accurate gifts of discernment and prophecy. Through revelation of the Holy Spirit, he knew that Ananias and Sapphira were deceiving him. They were acting presumptuously and in blatant disobedience toward the Lord. Satan had filled them with a lying spirit and spirits of jealousy, unbelief, pride and greed. While I know most demonic lies do not lead to the severe outcome of death, the unfortunate and deceitful actions of Ananias and Sapphira are a convincing scriptural example of the devastation that can occur when several demonic spirits are in operation. Let's investigate the spirits influencing this deception.

Spirit of Lies

This type of spirit speaks lies to and through its captive. As Ananias and Sapphira embraced the suggestion of Satan that they deceive the apostles, it was easy for them to stand before a man of God—and, actually, God Himself—and tell falsehoods without any fear of consequence. The fact that the lie was premeditated seems to make the deception even more appalling. Once a lying spirit has been welcomed, unashamed rebellion against the Lord and His standards will soon follow.

Spirit of Jealousy

This scene occurred during a time when the grace and graciousness of God was being expressed through believers. In particular, the Gospel of Christ was being proclaimed by Paul and John with great power. When a need arose among the believers, the Christians who owned property would sell it in order to meet the hardship and assist with the spreading of the Gospel.

We read in Acts 4:36–37 that a man named Barnabas sold a field he owned and placed the money he got for it at the apostles' feet. Agricultural land probably brought a good price. But it was the spirit with which Barnabas—the one known as the Son of Encouragement—gave that is noteworthy. He laid the money at the apostles' feet to help meet the needs of the lost and poor.

I surmise that Ananias and Sapphira grew jealous of Barnabas' favor and desired the same recognition. They sold their property and mimicked his humble posture in an effort to attain the same attention but without the sacrifice. Those operating under the influence of a spirit of jealousy will lash out at those used strongly by the Lord and will concoct any means to draw attention to themselves. Jealousy is easily threatened and is self-seeking and self-promoting.

Spirit of Unbelief

Ananias and Sapphira did not comprehend the benefits of sacrificial giving. When God directs giving, He will bless the obedience. The couple doubted they would receive sufficient recompense if they gave the full amount, so to ensure they were taken care of, they kept a portion of the profit.

Unbelief disregards God's faithfulness to those who serve Him sacrificially and with a pure heart. Unbelief does not accept the promises of the Lord; it causes those held captive by its lies to question the goodness, power and faithfulness of God's Word.

This spirit paralyzes faith. Those who are bound by it do not believe God for the possible or the impossible. They struggle to accept the love of the Father and to believe prophetic words concerning their destinies. Their thoughts are full of pessimism; they repeat continually in their minds and in their words the risks of following God. They do not believe that God will act for them, and they try to convince others of the same fears and doubts.

Spirit of Pride

The two walked in an alarming level of pride. They felt justified by the act of giving, were conceited in their opinion of this achievement and desired vainly to be acknowledged because of their gesture. They agreed to test the Holy Spirit. They were mocking the authority and power of our God. In their haughtiness, they attempted to sneak their lies and greed past God. This is the essence of pride.

A person trapped by pride is always in the business of defending and justifying. Conceit, vanity and an argumentative personality are very common. This individual thinks too highly of himself and his opinions and will go to great lengths to prove a point even without experience or knowledge. Pride is always right and never admits wrongs. It is easy to recognize that unbelief and pride often partner together. As we have noted, Scripture says, "Rebellion is as the sin of witchcraft, and stubbornness is as idolatry and teraphim (household good luck images)" (1 Samuel 15:23, AMP).

Scripture compares pride to idolatry and icons that bring good luck! The root issue of pride is focusing too much on "I," making oneself and one's opinions the idol or object of worship. It holds no regard for spiritual accountability, the truth of Scripture or the heart of the Father.

Spirit of Greed

Scripture says that "the love of money is a root of all kinds of evil. Some people, eager for money, have wandered from the faith and pierced themselves with many griefs" (1 Timothy 6:10). Note that money is not in and of itself evil; it is the *love* of money that is evil. This was the trap for Ananias and Sapphira—they loved money and became greedy. This is covetousness.

Scripture also says that a person who is filled with the love of money cannot serve God: "No one can serve two masters. Either he will hate the one and love the other, or he will be devoted to the one and despise the other. You cannot serve both God and Money" (Matthew 6:24). At that point, money has become the god. Chuck Pierce explains this in *Ministering Freedom from Occult Bondages* (Wagner Publications, 2004): "Money is good when it is a servant to us. However, we can become slave to its dominion. Then it truly is an evil eye."

In review, Ananias and Sapphira opened themselves to darkness by believing demonic lies of deception, being jealous of others' attention, refusing to have faith in the promises of God, thinking too highly of themselves and their actions, and loving money more than God. The evil spirits that plagued Ananias and Sapphira are still very active today and are exposed and dealt with in deliverance sessions on a fairly regular basis.

We continue now with other spirits commonly dealt with in deliverance ministry.

Common Demonic Issues

Some demons are encountered in deliverance ministry more frequently than others. The following list gives a quick overview of the activities and evil schemes of these demons and shows how they gain a foothold.

Fear

A spirit of fear usually enters through a traumatic event and will paralyze a person from advancing into all that the Lord has designed for him or her. An individual gripped with fear will suffer from various symptoms including fear of death, fear of the dark, fear of heights, fear of authority figures, fear of man, fear of rejection, fear of closed or narrow spaces and fear of the water. Nightmares and night terrors are also prevalent among those struggling with fear issues.

A person who struggles with fear issues is usually a "people pleaser" and has a difficult time saying no. He or she has trouble establishing boundaries and winds up living life based on the desires and needs of others. I have ministered to several individuals who were so overcome by fear, they were afraid to leave their homes. It is, as Scripture says, enslavement: "For you did not receive a spirit that makes you a slave again to fear, but you received the Spirit of sonship. And by him we cry, '*Abba*, Father'" (Romans 8:15).

Rejection

Rejection is by far the most common spirit I have dealt with in deliverance and inner healing ministry. Almost everyone I pray for has experienced rejection in one way or another. It can occur anytime from conception into adulthood. Remember that demons live up to their names, possessing those attributes and personalities. When a spirit of rejection is in operation, therefore, it causes the victim to be rejected on a repeated basis. The response that the person fears is the exact assignment and objective of this demonic being. The reality of never being accepted causes these individuals to behave in a manner that hastens the sad and discouraging outcome.

There are many causes of rejection. It can be a generational curse. It can come from a violent conception or disappointment about the conception or the manner of birth. It can happen when family members are emotionally, sexually or physically abusive. Other causes include: parents who are insensitive; classmates who were bullies; unfair, negative and critical teachers; being adopted; parents divorcing; a mother not bonding with her child after birth; a betrayal. Rejection can also be based on wrong perceptions, thought patterns and attitudes. The list is obviously quite extensive. This spirit is a major issue in the Body of Christ.

In *Evicting Demonic Intruders*, Noel and Phyl Gibson explain the fruit of rejection:

The roots of rejection produce three different fruit-bearing branches. Firstly, rejected people show a variety of aggressive attitudes. Secondly, they suffer from symptoms of self-rejection which may or may not be seen. Thirdly, motivated by their fear of rejection, they make constant attempts to avoid being rejected. The following lists clearly show the fruit systems:

Aggressive Reactions	Self-Rejection Symptoms	Measures to Counter Fear of Self-Rejection
Refusing comfort, rejection of others, harshness, hardness, skepticism, unbelief, aggressive attitudes, swearing, foul language, argumentativeness, stubbornness, defiance REBELLION Fighting	Low self-image, inferiorities, insecurity, inadequacy, sadness, grief, sorrow, self-accusation, condemnation, inability or refusal to communicate, fear of failure, fear of others' opinions, other fears, anxiety, worry, depression, negative attitudes, pessimism, hopelessness, despair	Striving, achievement, performance, competition, withdrawal, aloneness INDEPENDENCE Isolation, self-protectiveness, self-centeredness, selfishness, self-righteousness, self-justification SELF-IDOLATRY Criticism, judgmental attitudes, envy, jealousy COVETOUSNESS Self-pity PRIDE Ego, haughtiness, arrogance, manipulation, possessiveness, emotional immaturity, perfectionism

Heaviness

A spirit of heaviness is frequently tied to spirits of fear and rejection, forming a powerful three-strand cord. A person who is struggling with heaviness will exhibit depression, crying, self-pity, shame, sorrow, suicidal thoughts, unworthiness, victimization and other similar traits. Scripture says that those who mourn in Zion are appointed to exchange a spirit of heaviness for a garment of praise (see Isaiah 61:3, KJV).

A number of years ago the Lord gave me something of a crash course in dealing with the spirit of heaviness. It was during an International Congress on Deliverance Ministry held by Global Harvest Ministries in Colorado Springs. I was honored to join one of the leadership teams ministering to the participants. More than three thousand were in attendance, and ministry was open to all. Needless to say, the lines outside the ministry rooms seemed unending!

Prior to the meeting, I remember talking to Lord and saying, "Lord, I have dealt with a number of demonic issues on a repeated basis, but I have yet to deal with a spirit of heaviness. I need to learn about that one." Trust me when I say that you get what you pray for.

I found it curious that the first few individuals I ministered to had a stronghold of heaviness. By the end of the three days, I had prayed for more than twenty people bound by spirits of heaviness.

Those who are bound with a spirit of heaviness suffer from depression and sorrow. They find it difficult to have a positive outlook and to walk through life with joy, peace and victory. They struggle with a victim mind-set, believing they are always the victim and never the victor. Fear, rejection and heaviness often partner together in oppressing these victims. As I prayed for those twenty brothers and sisters, I watched their countenances be transformed before my eyes. They entered the prayer time with hopelessness, depression and despair, but as the Lord touched their lives, setting them free, they left in great peace and joy. Many, with tears of joy, expressed deep gratitude and sincere praise in their newfound freedom in Christ.

I thank the Lord for answering my request and helping me learn how to help set free those suffering from depression, fear, rejection and unworthiness. They came in crying and feeling like victims, but they were transformed into praising, joyful victors in Christ!

Infirmity

We mentioned earlier that Jesus healed a woman who had been bound physically by "an infirmity caused by a spirit (a demon of sickness). She was bent completely forward and utterly unable to straighten herself up or to look upward" (Luke 13:11, AMP). Before we move into our discussion concerning a spirit of infirmity, I want to state again that not all illnesses are caused by a demonic spirit. We live in a fallen world and have physical bodies that, if not taken care of properly, can become ill. Why some people are healed and others are not, I do not know. Still, when praying for healing, it does not hurt to deal with a spirit of infirmity. It is always wise to cover all the bases.

A captive of infirmity will suffer from disease, mental illness, a generational curse of infirmity, allergies, chronic health issues and so on. Those who have been involved in Freemasonry, college fraternities and sororities and any other secret society where allegiances are made to a pagan god or goddess in the initiation ceremony will almost always have a stronghold of infirmity. Those involved in witchcraft, cults or occult activities will suffer with major health concerns and often life-threatening diseases.

I recently prayed for Frank, a wonderful man of God who has served faithfully in ministry for many years. He had undergone an MRI that revealed two blocked arteries to his kidney. One had an 80 percent blockage and the other showed a 40 to 60 percent blockage. He was scheduled for further tests to confirm the doctor's findings and to determine the course of action to be taken in his medical treatment. Before the scheduled day of testing arrived, we prayed over the phone. It was a long-distance deliverance session.

As Frank shared with me details of his family history, it became clear that he was dealing with a generational issue of infirmity with roots in his ancestors' past involvement in occult and ungodly activities. He confessed and repented on behalf of his ancestors' sinful choices. Then in the name of Jesus we broke the spirit of infirmity and all ties linked to a spirit of witchcraft and an Antichrist spirit. I invited the Holy Spirit to fill every empty place with His presence—any and all areas where the house had been swept clean. Where there had been death, we spoke life. Where there had been illness, we spoke health. We released a submissive spirit to the Lord and asked for all the blessings He had designed for Frank.

The next day, Frank went for the scheduled test. What a faithful God we serve! Frank called, leaving a message of praise declaring the miracle God had performed. I also received the following report by e-mail:

> I just got home from the hospital. I went in to the cath lab and they looked for the blockages that the MRI showed my kidney to have. An 80 percent block on one and a 40 to 60 percent block on the other artery. When he injected the dye into my arteries, he checked each side three times and said, "Well, there are no blockages here at all, and you don't have any buildup in them, either."
>
> Praise the Lord! The curse is gone. These truly are days of freedom. Thank you for your prayers!

Perversion

We discussed sexual immorality extensively in chapter 5. When a lifestyle of whoredom, lust, fornication, adultery, homosexuality, pedophilia, bestiality, pornography, sexual promiscuity and the like is embraced, a spirit of perversion takes hold. Once a foothold is established, this demonic spirit fulfills its evil desires through the individuals it oppresses and influences.

This spirit is working overtime in our society—and is prevalent in the Church. There are many pastors and leaders, men and women in Christ, who are addicted to pornography and driven by lust. Families are being destroyed, husbands and wives are being driven apart and a door is being opened for future generations to be drawn into sexual addictions.

Those who are gripped by perversion and its accompanying sins keep their addictions secret. Shame and guilt harass, oppress and torment them, making it difficult for them to reach out for help. Some try to overcome this issue on their own without the assistance of a deliverance ministry team and the accountability of other brothers and sisters in Christ. But the reality is this: Sexual addiction is a demonic issue that requires the delivering power of Jesus and accountability toward other believers to walk in a life of purity.

If you are reading this book and are struggling with a stronghold of perversion, ask the Lord for forgiveness, submit yourself to the ministries of deliverance and inner healing, and establish accountability relationships to help you achieve freedom. Do not allow shame, guilt and embarrassment to keep you from getting help. God is a good God, and it is His desire to set you free.

It is equally important to throw out or destroy all objects that played a role in your connection with the spirit of perversion. These could be gifts from past sexual partners, movies with strong sexual overtones, music with lyrics focusing on sex, pornographic magazines—anything that is a reminder or a temptation must be removed. I know of many men and women who have thrown out their computers in order to remove the lure of Internet porn. Often drastic and radical measures must be taken to break the cycle of perversion and ensure victory over this dark spirit. No price is too great when choosing a lifestyle of freedom and purity in the Lord.

Witchcraft

Witchcraft refers to the attraction and the power of witches, black magic or sorcery. The Bible describes this encounter between Saul and the witch of Endor:

> Then Saul said to his servants, Find me a woman who is a medium [between the living and the dead], that I may go and inquire of her. His servants said, Behold, there is a woman who is a medium at Endor. So Saul disguised himself, put on other raiment, and he and two men with him went and came to the woman at night. He said to her, Perceive for me by the *familiar spirit* and bring up for me the dead person whom I shall name to you.
>
> 1 Samuel 28:7–8, AMP, emphasis added

Notice that Saul asks the witch to speak with the dead through a familiar spirit. A *familiar spirit* is an evil spirit believed to act as a servant to a witch. Actually, throughout Scripture witchcraft is referred to as a familiar spirit. It is this demonic spirit that operates through those involved in witchcraft, sorcery, magic, necromancy, etc. When the term *familiar spirit* is found in Scripture, therefore, it is synonymous with a stronghold of witchcraft.

Often when we think of witchcraft we get a picture of dark figures churning the cauldron and meeting in rituals to perform their demonic ceremonies, incantations and curses. Certainly people are involved in witchcraft at this level, but this spirit also presents itself in more common ways. Some of these are Ouija boards, horoscopes, Harry

Potter, zodiac signs, crystal balls, tarot cards, fortune-telling, palm reading, New Age meditation, séances and psychic powers.

Witchcraft is the counterfeit of the true power of the Son of God and the Holy Spirit. It is a spirit that functions in blatant rebellion. Witchcraft is a controlling spirit that functions completely opposite to purposes of the Lord. Because of this, witchcraft and an Antichrist spirit are often cohorts. When we participate in witchcraft practices—even in the simplest forms—we have embraced a familiar spirit. Even the popular slumber party game "light as a feather" is an open door to witchcraft. Any participation in witchcraft practices will hinder our relationship with the Lord. It is imperative to repent of any past or present involvement, stop all activity associated with it and throw out all items tied to it.

The symptoms of a familiar spirit are numerous, but the following are the most common: It is difficult to read the Word without experiencing confusion. Many people say that it feels as if a tight band is wrapped around their foreheads, and while reading the Word of God, the pressure increases, causing great discomfort. This spirit will block the ability to enter into the Lord's presence during worship or personal prayer time, thus preventing any spiritual growth. Many people suffer infirmities because of this demon. Witchcraft is a highly prevalent generational curse passed down the family line. It will continue to oppress the family line until it is plundered and evicted.

Currently a fierce battle is being waged on school and college campuses. Witchcraft groups such as Wicca are in the business of recruiting the youths of our nation into their fraternity. Young people are hungry for the supernatural, which has been missing from the church for quite some time. They want to experience power and be involved in something that has influence. Thus, they are susceptible to evil practices in order to fulfill this desire for power and to make an impact. The enemy is actively pursuing this next generation to thwart the move of God for which they were created. Parents must guard the activities of their children to protect their spiritual heritage and future.

Religious Spirit

A religious spirit is legalistic and controlling and will attempt to dominate spiritual settings. It attacks at a personal and corporate level. A person who has welcomed a religious spirit will be driven to perform religious tasks, believing that these actions will earn either human recognition, salvation or a greater reward in heaven. Even if the individual does not believe this doctrinally, his or her actions will prove otherwise. This spirit knows Scripture better than many believers and wants to be the center of attention. It opposes change and new moves of the Holy Spirit while desperately holding on to the old and familiar.

Many of those oppressed by this spirit feel certain that they have received salvation, but oftentimes there has never been a true conversion experience. We do not get saved by osmosis or by works! There has to be a moment when through faith and grace we invite the Lord into our hearts.

Bill was a faithful church member; he attended every service, prayer meeting and social function. And he knew the Word of God. He would come to every prayer meeting determined to read a lengthy passage of Scripture and then to give a ten-minute sermon. He was faithful to "share" even when he was not invited to do so. And Bill would pray. Not only would he pray, but he would pray long and hard, drawing all attention to himself and his agenda.

When the leaders of these meetings began to correct his dominating actions, Bill grew defensive, countering that God told him to behave in this manner. He explained that he was operating under the anointing of the Holy Spirit, and in his opinion the leadership did not have the right to question his actions. Bill's behavior made others feel they were not spiritual enough—or not as spiritual as he was. Actually, he enjoyed making others feel inferior. According to Bill, no one else had his or her spiritual life in order. You can imagine that Bill had a difficult time making friends and fitting into a church setting. People found him odd, offensive and difficult to deal with. I know no other way to put it: He oozed spirituality in a nauseating manner!

By this time, the leadership team of the church knew that he was influenced by a religious spirit. As months went by, we continued to pray and reach out to Bill with the love of the Lord. We desired to see him set free.

One night during a church meeting, God moved supernaturally in Bill's life. A powerful time of worship was drawing to an end, and the Holy Spirit was resting heavily on each of us. I noticed the Lord was touching Bill; he began to weep.

At the Lord's direction, I made my way to Bill and whispered, "Are you all right? What is God doing?"

Suddenly Bill shot out of his chair and fell to the floor in a full-blown demonic manifestation. He was rolling uncontrollably, banging his head on the floor. With no time to lose, the pastor and I dropped beside him, commanding the demonic manifestation to stop.

Then the pastor began to talk to Bill about the love of the Lord and the gift of salvation. Bill listened intently.

Finally he replied, "The Lord has been speaking to me about salvation all week. I thought it was for my family; I've been interceding for their salvation. What you are telling me is that the Lord was speaking to me about myself. You are right—I am not saved!"

Right there on the floor in this church meeting, Bill got saved and set free from a religious spirit. He leaped from the floor in celebration, shouting for joy in his newfound freedom in Christ. Bill's life was radically changed!

What Are Incubus and Succubus?

Both church and secular history make reference to the spirits of incubus and succubus. The tradition of the story suggests that before God created Eve, He first created a female being named Lilith from the animals and Earth. She was deeply in tune with her earthly surroundings and a free spirit. When Adam tried to procreate with her, she became enraged and moved to the area of the Red Sea. There she began to mate with demons and produced the demonic offspring of incubi and succubi.

The dictionary defines a spirit of *incubus* as a spirit or demon thought to lie on a sleeping person, especially on women, for the purpose of sexual intercourse. *Succubus* is defined as a female demon thought to have sexual intercourse with sleeping men. These visitations occur in the night hours and affect dream as well as physical activity. In many cases the individual thinks he or she is having a nightmare only to wake up and actually see and feel the demon in the act of sex.

These demons seem to be drawn to those who are lonely and desiring physical intimacy. They appear at first as a handsome man or beautiful woman. After several visits and in the act of intercourse, their true demonic identity is revealed, and the pleasurable sex act then becomes one of pain and aggression.

I once ministered to several women intercessors who had been praying together on a weekly basis for several years. They were all single and lonely, and greatly enjoyed their friendship with each other and the weekly times of intercession.

But they had a concern. They told me that each one of them was experiencing the same dream on a recurring basis. They said that in the dream, Jesus appears and begins to touch them physically and sexually. Because they were alone in life, they wondered if this was a gift from the Lord.

Nothing could be further from the truth. Our God would never touch any of His children in a perverse manner. Our union with the Lord is spirit to Spirit. It is never sexual. I explained the truth to these women, and they were horrified to realize they were entertaining demons. They repented for the open invitation to the demonic in their sex lives and were powerfully set free that day.

Another open door for a spirit of incubus and succubus is past involvement in New Age rituals, occultism and Satanism. Through meditation and various ceremonies these demons are summoned and received as spirit guides, forming a demonic alliance with the one who invited them in. When a pact has been made with darkness, demons do not like to give up their influence. Ministering deliverance to someone who has willingly received the sexual advances of these evil spirits in a covenantal ritual can be intense. But the blood of the Lamb and the authority of Jesus Christ always prevail.

Using Your Discernment

Discernment is a revelatory gift; it is through the Holy Spirit that this revelation flows. And since the use of this gift in deliverance ministry is to help set people free, we must always rely on the wisdom of the Lord and His loving guidance in using it.

It is absolutely vital that deliverance ministry be safe for the person seeking help. Anything that God reveals concerning another person must never be used to expose or embarrass that individual or be revealed outside the group without permission. There will be times, however, when you need the guidance and counsel of someone more experienced than you. In those cases, seek out a pastor, mentor or trusted spiritual leader relating to the revelation you think the Lord has given.

During my early training years under Alice Smith, I was on a team ministering to a young woman named Linda. The Lord was moving powerfully, and she was gaining great freedom in her life. We had met several times, and in each session the Lord revealed to me a hidden issue in Linda's family line. I knew she was unaware of it. It was very sensitive information, and I was not sure what to do with it. I *did* know that it was not correct to blurt it out without first submitting the revelation to the team leader. Following our third prayer time, I spoke privately with Alice about what I was discerning in my spirit. She told me that she had received the same revelation.

"What do we do with this?" I asked.

Alice replied, "It would devastate Linda to learn what the Lord is revealing to us. We will pray and break the power of this demonic scheme when we minister to her, but we will not blurt out names, and she will not have to know the full extent of this revelation."

That is exactly what we did, and Linda received complete freedom without facing more emotional damage in the process.

Along with the thoughts and ideas that the Lord speaks into our minds and spirits, sometimes He also lets us experience physical sensations that reveal information about demonic activity. To give you an example of how this works, I will share my experience with this kind of discernment, but please do not take this information and assume He works only in this manner. The Lord speaks to and through each of us differently. The most important thing to remember is to stay sensitive to the Holy Spirit and how He brings revelation into your life. You will soon learn to recognize physical sensations that are meant to impart information to you in ministry sessions.

This is how it often works for me: Sometimes my experience of a sudden, unexplained pain will be the trigger of discernment. This often means that the individual receiving prayer is struggling with a health issue caused by demonic influence or that there has been a past physical trauma. Many times the location of the pain reveals the origin of the condition. While ministering, for instance, I might experience a sharp sudden pain in my ear. When I mention this to the one receiving prayer, I might learn that he or she experienced a violent attack in which the ear was damaged. There are times when, in my spirit, I can hear the demons speaking their lies to the one I am ministering to. Sometimes I feel heat on my ears or hands, signaling an anointing for deliverance and healing. I have felt cold when I am in the presence of a spirit of death. When I am in the presence of witchcraft, I experience spinning or dizziness around my head, and many times it feels as if the ground is moving under my feet. Sometimes I "see" in my spirit the particular demon we are dealing with and its entry point. Sometimes I feel an overwhelming "knowing" in my spirit about an event. Sometimes I see in a closed vision—what I call my "mind's eye" or "spirit man"—the person suffering a traumatic event, and I know the demons attached to the incident by the nature of that revelation.

Thus far we have studied the importance of deliverance, the schemes of the enemy, our authority in Christ and how to diagnose demonic issues. Now we will take this foundational information and learn how to minister to the one bound by evil, from the first meeting to the place of complete freedom.

8

Setting the Stage for Ministry

"Then you will know the truth, and the truth will set you free."

John 8:32

In opening this chapter, I feel it is important for me to write a few words of wisdom to the new deliverance minister. Before any of us begin praying in deliverance ministry, we have to be walking in submission to those the Lord has placed in authority over our lives. Remember the story I shared in the introduction concerning the readiness of my family before praying in deliverance ministry?

We also have to go through a season of training under a deliverance ministry and submit to trained individuals. Why? We learn from those the Lord is using. Because they have gone before us, we learn from their successes and, more importantly, their failures. This will prove to be a powerful tool for both wisdom and protection when moving forward into the call of a deliverance minister. This does not mean that the Holy Spirit is not able to place us in situations in which He is the instructor. I know many deliverance ministers who had not planned on being involved in this form of ministry, but the Holy Spirit had other ideas. They did not go looking for it; it found them.

The strongest piece of advice I can give is to not become a lone ranger in the ministry of deliverance. Always stay within a network of those to whom you are submitted and who have the freedom to speak into your life's situations. I depend on certain individuals for spiritual guidance and counsel. I also have intercessors who pray for my husband, my children and me on a regular basis. I am always ready and willing to receive and listen to these wonderful praying partners. We all need those who will stand in the gap, interceding for protection, wisdom and the Lord's best. Not only do they help us see our own strengths and weaknesses, but their prayers place a protective hedge around us. This grows more important every day—not only from a warfare standpoint, but because of the growing reality of false accusations and lawsuits from those who are dissatisfied with deliverance ministry.

Using Wise Judgment

Why mention legal issues in a book on ministry? Because the possibility of a lawsuit by a dissatisfied "client" is far too real. I have several close friends who have been sued by those they ministered to. One lawsuit was initiated ten years after the ministry session. No laws were violated in that session, and no wrongful action occurred. It is a sad situation, but lawsuits are a customary practice in the United States. We should be informed in the event that legal action is taken against us.

I am not attempting to give legal counsel or advice. I am not a lawyer and do not carry legal credentials. I am a minister to the Body of Christ. Lawyers versed in the legal requirements and laws concerning ministry practices should be contacted to obtain legal counsel and advice. However, I do make use of a couple of practices in order to communicate clearly and to get all those involved on the same page.

Before I pray for someone, I send him or her a document that helps in the area of accountability. I clearly state that the ministry given and received is biblical, pastoral and spiritual counsel. It is not professional or medical counsel and should not be viewed as such. The individual receiving ministry agrees not to hold the ministry team, volunteers, directors or staff of the church or organization legally responsible for the outcome. While this document does not guarantee legal protection, it is a strong source of communication and provides understanding and accountability for all parties involved. It must be dated, signed and in my possession before the first ministry session. I keep these documents available for any future reference. Here are a few other points to consider.

Team ministry is the topic of chapter 9, but I would like to state here that team ministry provides safety for any deliverance minister. In the event of any false accusation, team ministry ensures that there is more than one witness to the truth.

Prayer ministers must always be careful concerning physical touch. Use wisdom when it comes to the laying on of hands. Ask first, and never touch anyone, especially a member of the opposite sex, in a manner that could be perceived as inappropriate. To be honest, I was once touched inappropriately by a prayer minister. It was not done with evil intent but with naïveté and inexperience. Because I knew the man who was praying for me, I knew that no harm was intended and simply told him to stop. He did so right away. I then took the time to explain the improper manner of the touching and gave a quick lesson on how to pray for someone appropriately at the church altar. Thank goodness this happened to someone who understood how to handle the situation. If not, this gentleman could have found himself in the middle of a lawsuit.

And finally, be aware of your civic responsibilities. While the information revealed in a session is confidential as far as the public is concerned, appropriate legal authorities are another matter. If you discover that you are ministering to an individual who is or has been involved in criminal behavior—such as murder, rape, child abuse or pedophilia—it is your legal, ethical and moral duty to report the offense to authorities. However, in these types of situations, facts need to be proven and verified before taking action. You will need to explain this information ahead of time to the one receiving prayer.

Now we begin.

Gathering Information

Deliverance ministry starts with an investigative phase. Before any sessions get under way, you will need answers to several questions from the person seeking help. At this point, I am interested in discovering if the problem really requires deliverance ministry. By asking certain questions and gathering information, I begin to understand how to move forward. Here are some questions that will help you bring the true problem to light. You will note that discernment is necessary from the very beginning.

"What Exactly Is the Issue?"

This is the first question that I ask. Why? Because many times what people think requires deliverance ministry does not. Trust me: Once people hear about your anointing and calling as a deliverance minister, phone calls will begin to flood in. Time becomes a precious commodity, so it is important to learn quickly when a situation really calls for deliverance and when it does not. The problem might be solved, for instance, by directing the person to qualified guidance counselors and praying over the phone.

I received a phone call recently from a young physician who had opened a private practice six months earlier. He was concerned because he had not attained the financial profit that he had projected for that short period of time. He was convinced that he was battling a generational curse of a spirit of poverty.

As I talked with him, it became evident that his personal finances were in great condition. Even so, because his medical practice was not producing large sums of money fast enough, he wanted me to break a spirit of poverty in order for blessing to come. In other words, he desired a swift solution.

I explained that he did not need deliverance but guidance from a financial or business consultant. I did pray, though, that God would bless his practice, instill patience in this eager young man and give him divine wisdom as his business grew and increased.

Sometimes you will discern that the battle is one of salvation. While working at Global Harvest Ministries, I received a phone call from Michelle, a young woman struggling with depression and a deep feeling of emptiness. She was certain that she needed deliverance.

I asked Michelle if she had ever received prayer concerning her depression and emptiness.

"Yes," she said, then added cautiously, "I have been through deliverance twice. Each time, I experienced some freedom, but after several days the depression returned and I was worse off than before. I know that I need help, but I am also a little nervous to submit myself to this process again. I am afraid that I won't be set free, that the battle will only intensify."

I responded, "I can certainly understand your hesitancy. Michelle, may I ask you a personal question concerning your relationship with the Lord?"

"Yes. Please, I welcome whatever counsel and wisdom you have to share," she replied.

Following the lead of the Holy Spirit, I inquired, "When did you invite the Lord to be Savior of your life? Do you know the moment this occurred?"

There was a long pause on the other end of the line. I waited quietly. Slowly she replied, "No one has ever asked me that before. I have been raised in church my entire life. I have always known of the Lord."

I explained that salvation does not take place by osmosis. Sitting in a church pew listening to and even recognizing the truth of Jesus Christ does not ensure eternal salvation. There has to be a moment when your life is surrendered to the Lord and He has been invited to be Lord and Savior. It does not have to be a dramatic event; it does not have to happen at a church service or spiritual conference. It can happen just with you and the Lord alone. The important point is that it has happened at some point in your life.

After several more seconds of silence, I could hear Michelle crying. Finally she confessed, "I am not saved. Can you please pray with me to receive salvation?"

Tears rolled down my cheeks as I led her through prayers of repentance and into a personal relationship with Jesus Christ. Before we hung up the phone, Michelle exclaimed happily, "I no longer feel empty. I feel joy, love and peace."

We both rejoiced, thanking the Lord for His goodness and faithfulness toward her.

"Have You Gone to Your Pastor?"

As I mentioned above, when you are active in deliverance ministry your time will be consumed by it if you are not careful. If the person seeking help is not part of your own church fellowship, find out if he or she is connected to a church that provides ministry to its members. If so, advise the person to seek help within the church. If not, encourage him or her to get involved in a local church. It is important to have the support of a spiritual family while walking through deliverance and inner healing.

What if the person goes to a church that does not believe in or practice deliverance ministry? This is very common; many churches still do not accept deliverance. If this is the case, I make myself available to the one seeking prayer, while also encouraging him or her to locate an active cell group or Bible study that understands and acknowledges the need for spiritual freedom from bondage. Spiritual support is crucial through this process.

"What Have You Done Thus Far?"

If you find out what the person has pursued thus far in his or her desire for freedom from bondage, you will get a pretty good sense of how successful deliverance ministry will be. Here is a good example of someone who was ready for prayer.

Joe was desperate for a breakthrough. He and his wife had had personal relationships with the Lord for more than five years. They were active in their church, attending weekly prayer meetings and Bible studies. Life was good.

Even so, Joe was plagued with demonic manifestations and attacks. Several years before coming to the Lord, he had had a desire for the supernatural and began practicing New Age meditation. He had hoped that it would fulfill his longing for the spiritual and draw him closer to God. During times of deep meditation, he had invited three spirit guides into his life.

Spirit guides are demons who appear as light, supposedly befriending the one who has invited them in. Their alleged assignment is to impart greater spiritual understanding and experiences. In reality they set a demonic trap resulting in great fear and bondage.

Because Joe had invited these demons to take up residence in his life, he was tormented on a consistent basis. He was particularly harassed during church services. Once he walked through the doors of the church, the spirits were constantly touching him and speaking to him. Desperate to be free, Joe had repented, prayed and renounced. He had destroyed all materials in his home pertaining to New Age practices and those demons. He had also approached his pastor for help. But because his church did not understand deliverance ministry, he was told simply to read the Bible and pray more.

Joe had done all he knew to do in an attempt to break the tie with these spirits. Finally he recognized that he needed a deliverance ministry team to help him receive freedom. Once he submitted himself to a team, the Lord moved powerfully, and he was set free in one short time of ministry.

When a person has repented, prayed, renounced sin and rebuked evil, or has done all that he or she knows to do, and the torment continues, it is time to seek deliverance ministry. Sometimes we need the anointing and agreement of prayer by others to gain absolute victory.

Let me mention, however, that some people will go from counselor to counselor with no intention of gaining freedom. These people usually attempt to instruct the deliverance minister on how to pray for and meet their needs. They then blame the prayer minister for their lack of freedom.

Use caution and seek the Lord before allowing a lot of your time to be stolen by those who have no real desire for help. Along with that, do not allow anxious individuals and the demons in operation to control your schedule. There are times when ministry will need to happen right away, but for the most part this is not necessary. From the start, establish healthy boundaries that promote confidence in your leadership ability and authority.

"Are You Willing to Stop Sinning?"

In the case above, Joe worked in cooperation with deliverance ministry to break the pattern of sin and strongholds. He had cut off all participation in sinful actions and truly desired to be set free. If, however, an individual submits to the deliverance process and is still actively engaged in sin, the breakthrough will not last. Actually, if a person invites the problem back after ministry, the latter state of the individual may be far worse, and much effort and time will have been wasted. I do not agree to pray with someone unless he or she is ready and willing to turn from active involvement in blatant sin. Thus, in the investigative phase it is crucial to find out if the individual seeking help is still involved in sin.

Pastor John called the U.S. Prayer Center office in Houston, Texas, where I served as assistant prayer coordinator, in urgent need of assistance. He had been ministering to a woman in his church by the name of Christina for five weeks. She was experiencing great torment, and demonic manifestations were occurring every night in her apartment. These visitations were frightening her and her three daughters. Being new to deliverance ministry, Pastor John had done all he knew in praying for Christina, but she could not gain freedom. He asked if I would help. I agreed, scheduled an appointment and secured the team members.

Pastor John and Christina arrived for the ministry session. Since the pastor and the church's deliverance team had been meeting with Christina for five weeks, I assumed that they had investigated all essential areas. Because of this, I did not ask some of the questions I normally do before agreeing to pray with someone. (I have since learned never to assume!) I did ask her to explain the torment she was experiencing. As I listened, I knew it was a stronghold of witchcraft with strong ties to voodoo practices.

The team began to minister to Christina. We prayed and asked the Lord to bring revelation of the root or pillar event that had opened a door to this stronghold of witchcraft. We asked Christina if she had been involved in witchcraft at any point in her life. What about past family members? We prayed through all these areas, broke ties and renounced in Jesus' name, but this spirit was not budging. Let me explain that I had assembled a power-packed team. We had all ministered together on a regular basis for several years, and it was not normal for spiritual freedom not to come quickly with this group. I could see it on the team members' faces, and I was beginning to feel it as well: We were stumped by this demon. It would not leave.

I then heard the Holy Spirit speak to me. *Becca, as I instruct, ask Christina the following questions.* After hearing each question in my spirit, I then voiced it to her. This had happened to me several times in previous deliverance sessions, so I knew the Lord was trying to expose something. The following dialogue transpired.

"Christina, what time of the night do these visitations happen?"

"Around midnight."

"They happen at the same time every night?"

"Yes."

"Are you and your girls asleep by this time?"

"Yes."

"Is there music playing in the house that would present an open door to these demons?"

"No."

"Are there items in your house that are attached to witchcraft or voodoo practices?"

"No."

"Christina, I will ask one more time, you have no clue why these spirits are tormenting you daily and entering your home every night and frightening your girls? You have not been in the past and are not presently involved in any type of activity that would allow this to be happening?"

"No."

"Well, Christina, the Lord wants you to tell me who is lying in bed next to you when the torment begins and the demonic visitations occur."

Christina's face instantly turned red. She raised her head, locked eyes with me and answered, "My boyfriend."

I responded, "Christina, the Lord wants you to tell Pastor John, the team members and myself how long you and your boyfriend have been living in sin. He also wants you to tell us the evil practices your boyfriend is involved with and performs in your apartment on a daily basis."

With an edge of defiance in her voice she replied, "We have been living together for two years, and he is a voodoo priest from Africa. He practices witchcraft in my apartment."

Needless to say, the group was stunned. I turned to the pastor and asked, "Pastor, did you have any idea this was happening?"

His face was nearly frozen in shock. "No, I did not."

"And how long have you been ministering to her?" I asked.

Now quickly growing agitated with Christina and the situation, he turned to look at her while answering my question. "Five weeks!"

I then confronted Christina. "How dare you waste five weeks of this pastor's time. How dare you waste two hours of my time. Do you know you are in blatant sin?"

"Yes."

"Then why have you submitted yourself for deliverance ministry?"

"Because," she said, "I was hoping to get breakthrough so I could continue to live with my boyfriend. He won't marry me, but I love him. I thought the deliverance might make my sin and the spirit of witchcraft easier to deal with."

I was truly shocked. "You have been using deliverance ministry to get enough temporary relief from the torment, in order to go home and purposefully sin, opening yourself up once again to this demon of witchcraft?"

With a shrug she said, "Yes."

"Christina, are you willing to repent, get right with God and break off the relationship with your boyfriend? You can do this right now. We can then pray and get you free from this torment and a life with a voodoo priest."

"No," she said. "I will not repent, and I have no desire to break the relationship with my boyfriend. I love him."

I announced immediately that the deliverance session was over!

I believe this episode is proof enough that it is imperative to find out if someone is involved in blatant sin, and, if so, will forsake it. I learned my lesson, and since that ministry session many years ago I have made this a top priority.

"Are You Willing to Cooperate with the Ministry Leader?"

Anyone seeking help must express willingness to co-operate with deliverance ministry. Try to get a sense of compliance in the early interview stage. Is he or she willing to complete homework assignments, for instance?

By the way, this may seem obvious, but it is imperative to talk to the one needing the ministry. Sometimes a friend or family member will call on behalf of someone else. An example is when a mother calls on behalf of a grown child requesting a ministry session, but the adult child is not willing

142

to make the personal contact. Ministry cannot be forced, nor can it be done by proxy. If the individual wants breakthrough, he or she can speak with you directly. It is a different matter, of course, if a parent is calling on behalf of a young child.

The point is that the one in the battle must desire deliverance and be willing to follow ministry leadership. The person has to be compliant in order to repent of, renounce and break free from the schemes of darkness. It is a choice to obtain and walk in freedom.

"Are You Receiving Ministry Elsewhere?"

If a person is already submitted to another deliverance counselor, I will not minister to him or her. It is not wise to receive counsel and deliverance ministry from more than one minister at a time.

Granted, it is possible to make an exception. If I am aware that an individual is being harmed by an unhealthy and scripturally unbalanced deliverance ministry, I will share my concern with the person and schedule a ministry session.

Preparation for the Deliverance Session

If you decide that the individual is ready for ministry, you must explain that walking through a season of deliverance and inner healing can be intense, even painful. Knowing what to expect helps in the mental, emotional, physical and spiritual preparation. People entering deliverance ministry may have to forgive those who caused them deep wounds. They must be willing to take on a new mind-set and determine to stand against demons as they try to regain entrance. They will also need new dedication to reading the Word of God and spending time in His presence. While the outcome is victorious, the path to get there will require a price.

When a deliverance session is scheduled, I assign homework. This promotes spiritual preparation and sometimes helps bring a fast and easy breakthrough. There are two great books that effectively aid this course of action. One is *Breaking the Enemy's Grip* by Eddie Smith (Bethany House, 2004), and the other is *Set Yourself Free* by Robert Heidler (Glory of Zion International Ministries, 2002). I strongly suggest that these books be purchased and read before the deliverance session. Each is a wonderful guide for the process. They are also great tools for those who are new to the idea of deliverance and need further understanding prior to receiving ministry.

Some people fast before coming to a ministry time. I do not require this, but I do recommend it. If the Lord leads the individual to fast, then it is important to obey. As the ministry time approaches, the warfare greatly intensifies. Situations will arise to keep the individuals from making their appointments. Harassment will increase, and fear of submitting to the deliverance team will begin to surface. I communicate this clearly ahead of time and tell the one in need of prayer to stand firm against these schemes. I also pray, binding and gagging the spirits of darkness, and ask the Lord for a hedge of protection until the scheduled time of prayer.

Forging Onward

Now that you have an idea of how ready the individual is, and you are ready to move forward into a scheduled time of ministry, it is time to contact those who will participate on the team. We will discuss in the next chapter the importance of team dynamics, including accountability, leadership multiplication and other areas important for a growing and effective deliverance ministry.

9

TEAM MINISTRY

Again I tell you, if two of you on earth agree (harmonize together, make a symphony together) about whatever [anything and everything] they may ask, it will come to pass and be done for them by My Father in heaven. For wherever two or three are gathered (drawn together as My followers) in (into) My name, there I AM in the midst of them.

Matthew 18:19–20, AMP

There is great authority in corporate prayer. When two or three come together in faith and commitment to Christ, He is there in the midst. This speaks of the greatness of our Lord. No one but God is omnipresent. The size of the assembly does not cause the Lord to move. The fact that there is unity places Jesus in the center of the prayer. It is this position of agreement that moves the hand of God. This reveals the importance of gathering together corporately and working together in the Body of Christ. Wherever and whenever believers come together in the name of Jesus, whether it is to honor, worship or serve, this gathering becomes a temple of God where the Holy Spirit dwells and is active.

For this reason, I am a strong advocate of team ministry. Team ministry provides an environment and atmosphere for the Holy Spirit to move. It is powerful and effective and provides hands-on training for others in preparation for leadership. As I invite people to pray on my teams, I consider each person's gifting. It is always helpful, for instance, to have someone with a sharp gift of discernment present. Strong prophetic and revelatory gifts are valuable. It is also effective to invite a team member who is motivated by mercy, to balance the straightforwardness of the discerner and prophet.

I want to mention again that it is not wise to place God in a box. I do not form ministry teams with the purpose of trying to fit this exact mold. It is helpful, however, to understand the importance of spiritual gifts and to utilize each team member to his or her fullest potential. By working together, the team members will begin to function as a unified body, which invites the presence of the Holy Spirit.

Use Prophetic Revelation Wisely

It is a powerful experience to watch the Lord move through team members in the area of prophetic revelation. For this very reason—the desire to hear from the Lord—I intentionally do not reveal a lot of information to the team members when they are invited to participate. I encourage each of them to pray and intercede, and come prepared to reveal what the Lord has spoken. I also tell the person receiving ministry that I have not disclosed the particular issue or any personal information to team members.

It is encouraging and faith building as prophetic revelation is released. The Lord will reveal one layer of deception to one team member and another layer of deception to another team member. As the strategy unfolds, we are all aware that the agenda for the deliverance time has been set by God and not our own human thoughts and patterns. The team is then encouraged to work together in unity, and powerful breakthroughs are achieved. In the anointing of the Holy Spirit and in the name of Jesus Christ, strongholds are plundered.

Prophetic revelation is also important for revealing those issues and demonic influences that attempt to remain hidden. What do I mean by this? More times than not, there will be an issue that the person receiving prayer is not aware of.

Let me stop right here and clarify. I am not speaking of "planting a memory" in someone's mind. As deliverance ministers, we should not be in the business of telling people they have been sexually abused or satanically ritually abused if there is no valid proof. I have prayed for more damaged individuals concerning memories placed in their heads by deliverance ministers and Christian counselors than for people who have actually been sexually abused or involved in Satanism. I have also seen parents falsely accused and families destroyed by erroneous "revelations." We must weigh insights very carefully before spouting off incorrect prophetic insight. Remember, if a demon tells you something happened to the person in the past, the demon's father is Satan, and he is the father of lies! Is it possible demons set us up to believe the lie in order to kill, steal and destroy? Absolutely. We need to move in the wisdom and discernment of the Lord when it comes to dealing with insights for which there is no proof.

Let's get back to hidden issues. I am referring to the fact that spirits may have attached themselves to an individual through a traumatic event that the person has forgotten.

Once it is revealed, however, the person regains memory of it. There will be no need to convince the individual that the event was real. He or she will know.

George had been struggling with an overwhelming generational curse of witchcraft. He also had a problem submitting to male authority figures in his life, which threatened job security and family relationships. The battle was intense. He was desperate for breakthrough. As our team ministered to George, the Lord was prophetically revealing key strategies to set George free.

Several minutes into the ministry session, we came to a standstill. We prayed, asking the Lord to bring further revelation. In my "mind's eye," I saw a scene of George as a young boy with a man whom I felt sure was his uncle. George had walked into a room where his uncle was engaged in witchcraft practices that involved black spiders. Upon seeing George enter the room, the uncle began to harass and terrify him with the black spiders.

I barely finished relaying the revelation when George cried out, "I remember! I was seven years old. That event terrified me." The team prayed and broke the power of the event over George's life. We led him through prayers of inner healing, asking the Lord to wash over George's emotions and to shatter the walls this traumatic event had placed around his heart, preventing him from relating to men. George was powerfully healed and set free.

Always Have a Leader Present

Every deliverance team must have a team leader. Somebody has to have the final authority, and the team members must be willing to submit to this leadership. In return, those who partner with a leader should be valued, appreciated, respected and esteemed. They should leave their time under leadership stronger in the Lord.

The team leader oversees all that is happening. This is not a matter of control but of equipping and training. True leaders empower those in their sphere. They desire to see the anointing and gifting of those submitted to them released. This does not negate the need for instruction or even correction, but when this does happen it is done in the wisdom of the Lord with emotions under control. Leaders should never use their authority to demean someone or flex their spiritual muscles. Leaders are to have the heart, attitude and actions of a wise servant.

If you have the opportunity to lead a team, remember these leadership attributes. With them, building teams and ministry partners is easy. People will seek you out for mentoring and guidance and will remain loyal and faithful to the vision.

Beware of Dangerous Traps

Deliverance is frontline ministry. We need to be aware of snares. How? By listening to the wisdom and discernment of the team members. In this way a formidable wall of protection is formed that is difficult for the enemy to penetrate. Here are three particularly devious traps. Team ministry can alleviate them.

Praying for Members of the Opposite Sex

It is never appropriate for a man to minister alone to a woman or a woman to minister alone to a man—especially when the problem to be dealt with is sexual in nature. The enemy will use the opportunity to create an open door of physical attraction between the two parties. More often than not, an affair will be the outcome. Even if the counseling and ministry is handled appropriately, the appearance of the meeting can cause rumors and accusations that will damage reputations.

Witchcraft Infiltration

Witchcraft infiltration is another area of caution. I am not saying that we are to grow suspicious of every new person and face, but be aware that people will infiltrate teams in order to bring confusion and destruction.

I have witnessed firsthand the harm and devastation that accompanies one who is functioning under the control of a witchcraft spirit. This person will have the ability to receive revelation, but it comes from spirits of darkness, not the Lord. Many times this person will share supposed words of wisdom or knowledge, but they will not be edifying or encouraging. In fact, they may lead to fear or legal repercussions. The person will have an air of spiritual superiority that no one else can achieve, an impression that he or she is the only one with all the answers. The ministries that this person has infiltrated will go through a season of crisis, threatening the purposes that the Lord has called them to fulfill.

Jezebel Spirit

First Kings 16:29–22:40 tells the story of Ahab, Jezebel and Elijah. The spiritual ramifications of this story continue today.

Ahab was a wicked king—perhaps the most wicked ever to lead Israel. He married Jezebel, daughter of the king of the Sidonians, and soon joined in her worship of Baal, the male god of power and sexuality. The pagan worship included tributes to Asherah, the female goddess of fertility, love and war. The rituals were filled with depraved sexual practices. Jezebel was a fanatical worshiper of these demonic deities. The Israelites were following her gradually into destruction.

God raised up the prophet Elijah to stand against this apostasy. He was a reformer sent to reestablish the covenant between God and the Israelites, and he had several dramatic encounters with Jezebel and her false prophets. Jezebel was in the business of killing off the Lord's prophets and threatened Elijah. She wanted nothing to stand in the way of worshiping Baal and Asherah. This spirit is still alive and active today, attempting the same scheme.

As with witchcraft, a person operating under this spirit will infiltrate churches, prayer groups and ministries. The person will attempt to get close to leadership quickly. Because of the ability to manipulate with smooth words, the person usually receives great favor, and the discerning voices of other trusted relationships will be dismissed. This individual will show great loyalty in the presence of leadership, but work quietly behind the scenes to cause division and dissension. This spirit will seek promotion and will attempt to take those out of leadership roles who pose a threat. Ministries that this spirit seeks to destroy are the ones flowing in the power of the Lord and speaking forth prophetic truths.

We have to be cautious not to confuse immaturity with a Jezebel spirit. Falsely accusing someone of a Jezebel spirit is the same as taking on the characteristic of this entity, which is a murderous spirit.

If team members remain approachable and teachable, they can hold back any infiltration. If, however, the team arrives at a place that does not tolerate correction, or if it is threatened by the wisdom and spiritual insight of those who partner with it, then it has issued an invitation for attack. We must use discernment. This is why team ministry is so crucial. We need each other and the confirmation of the Holy Spirit in order to guard against all ploys of the enemy.

Leadership Multiplication

No man is an island. What God has imparted to leaders should be given freely to those who partner with us. The days of ministry and church being a "one-man show" no longer exist. God is establishing new order and vision in this hour, with an emphasis on mentoring and discipling a new generation of leaders. I am a firm believer in mentoring and discipleship. All spiritual parents should produce spiritual children.

In a growing, thriving Spirit-led deliverance ministry, more team leaders will be needed in order to handle the increase. Team ministry is key in the training, equipping and positioning of new leaders to partner in the vision. Once healthy reproduction has begun, it will continue. The result will be a strong, empowered and reputable leadership team with sharp, authoritative and effective ministry.

10

How to Conduct
a Ministry Session

For our struggle is not against flesh and blood, but against
the rulers, against the authorities, against the powers of
this dark world and against the spiritual forces of evil in
the heavenly realms.

Ephesians 6:12

Now it is time to engage in deliverance ministry. I will base
this teaching on work with a ministry team, as opposed to
one-on-one ministry. As I stated in chapter 9, the teams that
I lead are prophetic in nature. They lean on wisdom gained
through experience, but depend on the anointing of the
Holy Spirit. I am awed every time I witness the powerful
delivering hand of the Lord move graciously on behalf of
His children.

This chapter will focus on how to conduct a ministry session. Always keep two things in mind: One, each team member is uniquely gifted and should minister in the calling the Lord has placed on his or her life; and, two, it is important not to limit God to this or any method. Follow the guidance of the Holy Spirit and allow Him to set the agenda for each deliverance session. Here, then, are steps that have proven to be effective in a ministry setting.

1. Create the Right Environment

When a team I am leading meets with a ministry recipient for the first time, we begin with introductions and getting to know one another. This includes explaining to the recipient how the ministry time will progress. Here are points to make:

The recipient's job is to receive from the Lord. The team will do the work. I encourage the individual to share anything he or she is feeling and hearing throughout the session, but I stress the importance of resting in the peace of the Lord while being ministered to. Why is this important? Because some people want to control their ministry time instead of allowing the Holy Spirit to be in charge.

The ministry time will remain confidential. This is very important. When someone has submitted to ministry, it should be a place of safety and trust. Sensitive information will be revealed, and for the team to disclose anything from the sessions with others outside the prayer team—other than appropriate legal authorities—is not ethical.

The team will probably make use of the practices of laying on of hands and praying in the Spirit. If the recipient is new to this kind of ministry setting, I want to help prepare him or her. I have never had anyone oppose these actions. Up-front communication opens the way for the individual to be more receptive to ministry. We should reach out in a manner that opens doors for new spiritual experiences.

Manifestations might occur. I explain that if this happens, the team members will speak in a strong, authoritative manner. The recipient needs to understand that the aggression is directed toward the tormenting evil spirit, not him or her. I explain that any evil demonstrations and outbursts will be dealt with quickly in the name of Jesus, and I encourage the individual to not be afraid. The Lord and the ministry team will battle on his or her behalf.

All prayers should be spoken audibly. Spirits of darkness might be able to place evil thoughts in our minds, but they cannot read our thoughts. They gauge the success of their schemes by viewing our words and actions. When dealing with the demonic realm, therefore, all prayers and directives must be voiced out loud.

I then ask the one seeking prayer to share some of his or her struggles, battles and concerns with the team and me, but not in great detail. Remember, I want to give room for the Holy Spirit to bring prophetic insight and words of knowledge and wisdom. At this time, if the team members feel it appropriate to share all the Lord has revealed to them, they do so. But sometimes it is better to wait until an appropriate time in the session. This helps break the power of the open door to the demonic once it is revealed by the Lord to the team members.

2. Open with Prayer

Now is the time to invite the presence of the Holy Spirit. As I begin, I submit myself, the other team members and the ministry recipient to the Lord and His agenda. I ask the Lord to place a hedge of protection around each of us in the room and our family members. I pray for blessings, for increased anointing and for the Lord to send His warring angels to guard every corner of the room as we pray.

The following is an example of how I would open in prayer. In this case, the ministry recipient is named Candy—actually a composite of people I have prayed for—and the ministry team members are Mary, Joan and me.

> Father, I thank You for this time together and for the opportunity to minister to Candy. Lord, I ask that Your presence and anointing will rest on Candy, Mary, Joan and myself.
>
> Lord, I lift up Mary and pray that an anointing for deliverance and revelation will rest on her. I pray for a hedge of protection to be placed around her, her husband and her children. Lord, I thank You for her willingness to serve and to minister to those who are bound by darkness. Thank You for her sensitive heart and spirit. I pray a special blessing over her today as we minister.
>
> Father, I thank You for Joan. What a special friend and sister in Christ! I thank You for her obedience toward You and her servant's heart. Place a wall of fire of protection around her and her husband as we minister. Lord, increase her gift of discernment, and may she speak forth the sharp and precise revelation of the Holy Spirit that will bring freedom for Candy.
>
> Father, I thank You for the privilege of setting the captive free. Thank You for the calling You have placed on my life. I pray that You will use me today and that I will hear Your agenda for Candy. Lord, I need Your anointing and ask for and receive it right now in Jesus' name.
>
> On behalf of the team, I admit we have nothing to offer in and of ourselves. We recognize that anything we have to give that brings freedom comes from You, Your Son and the Holy Spirit. We are empty and poured-out vessels and ask today that You will fill us with Your wisdom, revelation and discernment. Lord, we ask for a spirit of revelation and prophecy to rest in this place. And right now we thank You for this anointing.

Father, we pray now for Candy. May You bless her and her family today. We ask for a wall of fire of protection around her now. Father, she has been through an intense battle and is in need of freedom. We thank You, Lord, for her willingness to submit to this process. Thank You for her sweet spirit. And Lord, I sense the love that You have for this precious sister and the desire You have to set her free. Thank You, Lord, that You will battle on her behalf today and prove Yourself faithful in setting her free from this oppression. Station Your warring angels in every corner of this room as we minister. Holy Spirit, I invite You right now to flow over Candy with Your peace and love from the top of her head to the bottom of her feet. Bring an anointing for deliverance and inner healing.

And I announce right now to all spirits of darkness that are tormenting my sister that your agendas are being plundered, cancelled and broken today in Jesus' name.

It is not necessary to follow this exact model of prayer; it is meant to give an idea of how to move forward.

Remember, this is warfare. We always address demons in an authoritative manner. Praying with your eyes open signifies influence over evil spirits and also keeps you aware of what is happening. Even through the opening prayer, my eyes remain open and on the one receiving ministry. Oftentimes, the things I am praying will trigger a response from the evil spirits that I need to be aware of.

3. Wait: Listen for Revelation from the Lord

Now that the presence of the Holy Spirit has been welcomed into the ministry setting, it is time to listen to His voice. Take the time to sit quietly in His presence in order to receive direction as to how to proceed.

In the opening conversation with the group, Candy revealed that she was in a desperate place and needed a spiritual breakthrough. She shared that she came from a rough childhood home, and that memories from her past haunted her, preventing her from walking a life of freedom and victory. She said she was hindered emotionally, and at night she suffered from nightmares that relived the trauma from her past. Here, then, is an example of how revelation from the Lord might be handled:

BECCA: Candy, I am sensing that your relationship with your mother was extremely strained. Actually, what I believe the Lord is showing me is that your mother was a very depressed woman suffering from alcoholism. As a result, she was emotionally and verbally abusive. Is this right?

CANDY: Yes. My mother had a very difficult childhood and was a very depressed woman. She drank continually. She was not a nice drunk and yelled at us kids on a fairly regular basis. Nothing we did was ever good enough or right. My childhood home was not one of joy and peace, but of pain and tears.

BECCA: Thank you for sharing this with us. Does anyone have further revelation at this time?

JOAN: I see that because of your mother's actions you suffer greatly with a spirit of rejection, heaviness and fear. Do you agree with this?

CANDY: Yes.

BECCA: Okay. We are going to begin praying through this revelation. Candy, you rest in the peace of the Lord while we pray and begin to deal with these issues.

When sharing a revelation, there will be times that we hit the mark and times that we do not hit the mark. Even so, we grow by communicating the impressions we think we are getting. If we take the risk and speak up and do not get it right, then we continue to pray, asking the Lord for further revelation. No one is 100 percent accurate all the time.

4. Ask the Lord to Reveal the Root or Pillar Event

The *root* or *pillar event* is the original traumatic episode in which the spirits of darkness gained entrance. I have prayed for numerous people who have gone through deliverance and inner healing but still suffer. The common complaint is, "I gained freedom, but it was not complete. After a couple of weeks, it was as if I had never gone through deliverance at all." In these cases, the root had not been successfully plucked out.

It is like pulling weeds. In order for the weed not to grow back, the entire root has to be dug up. If not, it will produce life again, and you will be back outside working the flower bed within a couple of weeks. Likewise, in deliverance, if the foundational or pillar event is not uprooted and destroyed in Jesus' name and the void places are not filled with the anointing of the Holy Spirit, then complete freedom will not be realized.

Let's return to Candy's ministry session. And remember that this is an example with experienced deliverance ministers. Don't be discouraged if the prophetic revelation you receive is not as detailed as the examples given in this chapter. Many things can be learned by asking questions; many times, that is how I discover what is needed.

BECCA: Father, thank You for the revelation You have released concerning Candy's mother. Lord, we ask that You will reveal the root event that caused the open door for heaviness, rejection and fear to enter Candy's life.

MARY: Candy, I am seeing that there was one night when you were a young child and your mother totally lost her temper, became violent, slapping you and throwing you onto the floor. You were injured in this violent episode. Actually, I believe that this was the first emotional and physical encounter with your mother. Is this correct? Did this happen?

CANDY: Yes. I was five years old. My mother was drunk and sitting in her favorite chair, crying. I tried to comfort her, but when I did, she became very angry and began yelling. I apologized and tried to leave the room, but she grabbed me and hit me violently several times. Finally, she threw me down onto the hardwood floor, and in the fall my wrist was broken. I could see the grief on her face concerning her actions, but to this day she has never apologized to me. This memory is so real that it seems and feels as if it just happened yesterday. I have a difficult time getting it out of my mind. This scene haunts me.

JOAN: That night as you were lying in your bed, alone in the dark crying, did a demonic spirit visit you?

CANDY: Yes, it did. I was so traumatized. After I got home from the hospital, I was left alone in the dark in my bedroom. Neither my mother nor my father came to comfort me, and my brother and sister stayed away for fear of making Mother angry. I felt an evil presence in my room, and I was overcome by fear. I have been afraid since that moment.

5. Move into Forgiveness

At this point, we would lead Candy in a time of forgiving her mother. By choosing to forgive, Candy is no longer controlled by her mother or the horrible events and memories of her past. This is vital: Forgiveness breaks the hold that hurtful people and situations have on our lives. We discussed forgiveness in chapter 5, but I want to mention here the importance of confessing, repenting of and releasing any harbored anger, bitterness or blame toward the abuser and God.

Many times when people suffer through situations such as the ones Candy endured, they are angry at God, blaming Him for the hurt and pain. Their thoughts go like this: *How could God have allowed this to happen to me? If He loved me, why didn't He protect me?* The Bible teaches that our God is a loving Father. His love is deeper and more vast than we can ever fathom. He allowed His Son to die in our place. We are His children, and He is grieved whenever we are harmed. We have to come to the realization that the bad things that happen in our lives are not God's fault. He is not the one to blame. Now is the time to express sorrow for being angry and bitter toward the Lord.

The truth is we live in a fallen world. On the one hand, the enemy and his demons work relentlessly to influence us toward evil. On the other hand, we have free will, and when we choose to turn from God and embrace that evil, the result is sin. It is through these sinful behaviors that deep hurts, wounds and terrible abuses happen—even toward those who are innocent.

Is the action of an abuser allowable? Absolutely not. In the cases of abuse, sexual molestation, rape, murder and so on, the violator must be held accountable for the evil and violent behavior.

And remember: Forgiveness does not mean that the ministry recipient now has to build a relationship with the abusive person. Never recommend any action that would endanger the one receiving prayer.

6. Bind the Strong Man and Plunder His House

Deliverance ministry is often compared to peeling an onion: You have to go through many layers before arriving at the core—and gaining freedom. Once the root issue and strong man have been revealed, then, as Scripture directs, the strong man must be bound and his house plundered: "How can a person go into a strong man's house and carry off his goods (the entire equipment of his house) without first binding the strong man? Then indeed he may plunder his house" (Matthew 12:29, AMP).

In Candy's case it was quite evident that she was struggling with spirits of fear, rejection and heaviness. In praying for her, I bound the strong man of fear and plundered all the activities and spirits attached to it. Here is an example of how I prayed:

> Spirit of fear, you have been exposed, and the finger of God is coming against you this hour. In the name of Jesus, I bind and gag you and command you to be silent and still. Your house is being plundered this day, and your assignment in Candy's life will be broken in the power of Jesus Christ.
>
> I break all ties between a strong man of fear and fear of man right now in Jesus' name. I break the tie between fear and fear of the dark in Jesus' name. I break the tie between fear and fear of rejection right now in Jesus' name.
>
> I break the generational curse of fear, and I sever all ties between Candy and her mother, her mother's mother and father, their mothers and fathers all the way back to Adam and Eve, in Jesus' name. I sever all ties of fear between Candy and her father, his mother and father, their mothers and fathers all the way back to Adam and Eve right now, in Jesus' name.

In a case like this I would continue to pray through all the issues associated with a spirit of fear that were present in Candy's life, being sure to address and break all generational curses that had been passed down by ancestors. Notice all the authority is in the name of Jesus. It is in His name that demonic assignments are broken.

Why do I deal with ties all the way back to Adam and Eve? This assures me that all past generations have been dealt with successfully. It never hurts to be thorough.

Once the spirit of fear has been plundered, it is time to address heaviness and rejection. They would each be dealt with and plundered in the same manner as the spirit of fear. I would then break the power of this three-strand cord in Candy's life. All ties between fear, heaviness and rejection would be cut off and each strong man cast out in the name of Jesus.

A good indicator that the demonic house needs to be plundered is when the strong man is commanded to leave and it still has grounds to stay. Once the house is ransacked, the strong man has nothing left to hold on to or to gain strength from.

Do I handle all ministry settings in this fashion? No. I pray as the Holy Spirit leads. There are times when a strong man is rebuked in Jesus' name and it leaves instantly.

7. Lead a Time of Confession and Repentance of Sin

Confession and repentance of sin break the back of the enemy. Why? Taking responsibility for sinful action brings it into the light of Jesus Christ. It is then washed clean by the blood of the Lamb and erased from the record, never to be found again. The enemy hates it when sin has been washed clean by the blood of the Lamb. Even so, people sometimes find it hard to let go of their sins. As suggested in point 5 above, Candy would need to confess and repent of anger, unforgiveness and bitterness—not only toward her mother but also toward her father since she viewed him as weak and unwilling to protect her.

In order to discuss another aspect of confession and repentance, let's leave our example with Candy for a moment.

I want to tell you Tina's story of the power of sin and the greater power of repentance.

Tina had been plagued with a spirit of perversion and had been bound to sinful sexual practices. But she had submitted to a season of deliverance and inner healing, and those of us who knew her were witnessing her transformation right in front of our eyes. She was close to complete freedom. Her husband, Glenn, was thrilled with the changes in his wife. Their marriage was being healed and restored. In addition, they were actively involved in a church cell group and building new and strong relationships of accountability with the cell group pastors, Craig and Anne.

Then one morning in the early hours, the phone rang at the home of Craig and Anne. Half asleep, Craig answered to hear Tina in a state of panic.

"Craig," she cried, "please, I need you and Anne to come over to my house right now! I am being tormented by demons. Glenn is out of town. I am all alone and I'm terrified! Please hurry!"

Craig and Anne bolted out of bed, grabbed whatever clothes were handy and drove to Tina's house. They sat up with her the rest of the night, praying over her. Tina was so terrified of what she was seeing and hearing in the demonic realm that she was unable to function normally. None of the prayers brought comfort.

Later that morning several of the church pastors were called to assist. They prayed for several hours and still were unable to relieve her state of terror. That night Craig and Anne brought Tina to church, hoping that the worship would calm her down. But the presence of the Lord seemed to magnify her condition.

The pastors approached me and asked if I would minister to Tina, who was then in one of the pastor's offices. I quickly grabbed two of my faithful ministry team warriors, and we made our way to Tina. This poor sister was in total fear. She was shaking and trembling and was barely able to speak. We began to minister to her, but the spirits were not responding.

I asked for a fuller account of the past twelve hours, and then sat down in a chair facing Tina. Following the leading of the Holy Spirit I asked, "Tina, what did you do last night to open yourself up to this torment? What do you need to repent of?"

She broke into deep sobs, making it difficult for her to speak. After some time, she replied with tears, "A demon entered my room and began to remind me of the pleasure of my past sinful life. I tried to stand, but the pull toward the temptation was too strong. I gave in and went onto the pornographic websites that I used to visit. I participated in online sex. As soon as I did this, that demon came back—and the torment is unbearable."

I instructed Tina to repent of this sin. As soon as she repented, we cast out the spirit of perversion and all the new cohorts that had joined in the scheme. Tina was instantly and miraculously set free. Having learned the lesson the hard way, she left that session committed to walking out her freedom and has never embraced this sexual sin again.

I also want to point out that if the confessed sin involved harm and pain toward another individual, then restitution may need to be made. Restitution is not always required if the one on the receiving end is unaware of the committed sin. I have seen this happen, and it can be awkward at best. In these cases, wisdom must be used. Restitution should be handled in a manner that brings restoration. Remember the wisdom of the team. If the team agrees that restitution is required, you might help direct the individual to further action.

8. Do Not Express Too Much Compassion

It is imperative in deliverance that we love the person but hate the schemes of the enemy. Be aware, however, that too much compassion by team members can sometimes interfere with the outcome of complete freedom. Let me show you what I mean.

Prior to salvation, Don had been involved heavily in occult practices. Because of the pacts he had made with spirits of darkness, the battle to gain freedom was proving to be intense. The team had been praying for Don for a couple of hours, but the familiar/witchcraft spirit was not budging. We felt certain we had covered all the necessary bases for evicting this evil spirit. I began to wonder what was happening.

My attention was drawn to Mike, who was sitting off to the side of the ministry team. He had asked to come into the session to learn about deliverance ministry, and I had agreed to let him observe. I noticed that tears were rolling down his cheeks; he was having a difficult time watching Don press in for his freedom. In fact, Mike expressed compassion at every demonic outburst. I realized that his concern was being directed toward the manifestation and not Don. The demon was able to use Mike as a legitimate sympathizer for its cause and refuse to accept the commanding authority of Jesus.

I quietly went over to Mike and asked him to leave the room, telling him I would explain later. As soon as he left, we commanded the spirit to go, and it obeyed immediately. In deliverance ministry, compassion has to be directed toward the right cause.

9. Be Prepared for Demonic Manifestations

Manifestations happen in deliverance ministry. Before addressing a demon, I command it to be bound and gagged. Most ministry sessions are calm with few or no manifestations, but outbursts do occur. Actually, I know of no deliverance minister who has not encountered a demonic manifestation at some point.

I served on the altar ministry team at a conference many years ago. Jennifer was a young woman in her early twenties who attended this gathering for the purpose of being set free from the demonic oppression that was plaguing her life. She was battling with unbelief and experienced great difficulty reading the Bible and hearing the true Word of God. Many times she found herself fighting off sleep in corporate gatherings and in her personal times with the Lord. I made myself available to her during the altar ministry times. She gained quite a bit of freedom over the first two days of the conference.

During the final altar ministry session, I prayed for Jennifer one last time. As soon as I laid hands on her, she instantly fell limp against my body. Her head was on my shoulder, and she was snoring in my ear! She was snoring so loudly that the other ministry team members began to look my way and chuckle. The obvious conclusion was that Jennifer was influenced by a spirit of slumber. It is mentioned in Scripture several times. The following verse describes the effect of being bound by this demon: "This is the reason that I speak to them in parables: because having the power of seeing, they do not see; and having the power of hearing, they do not hear, nor do they grasp and understand" (Matthew 13:13, AMP).

Needless to say, I quickly rebuked that demon and commanded it to leave in Jesus' name. As soon as I issued the decree, the spirit left. Jennifer came to abruptly, stood up, smiled and began shouting with joy, "It's gone! The spirit is gone! Thank You, Lord, I am free!"

Remember, this is warfare, and demons can and do use the bodies of their hosts to make themselves known. When dealing with a manifestation, we command it to stop in the name of Jesus, but we have to keep in mind that demons are rebellious beings. As we saw earlier, even when Jesus commanded an evil spirit to be quiet and come out, the Bible tells us it left with a shriek (see Mark 1:25–26). If they rebelled against His authority, they will rebel against ours. Here is a list of some of the more common demonstrations that occur in deliverance ministry:

Crying
Trembling
Fear toward the ministry team
Nonhuman voices
Strange facial expressions
Burping
Gas
Diarrhea
Vomiting
Coughing
Yawning
A mocking laugh
Contorted body positions
Perverse body movements
Quoting of Scripture (some demons know the Bible better than we do)
Screaming
Cursing
Motionless stupor
Unwillingness to look at the ministry team
An argumentative spirit
Playacting
False tongues, which are many times spoken to the team members in a disrespectful and aggressive manner
Threats made to the team members

Often I will direct the person getting prayer to open his or her eyes and look into my eyes. The evil spirits hate this and stubbornly attempt to look away. I command them to stop. Then I look those spirits right in the eye and tell them to leave in the name of Jesus.

Sometimes in desperation not to lose its hold, a demon will manifest and take you on a rabbit trail in an attempt to get the focus off itself. Demons are deceivers and liars, and I do not recommend conversing with them. God is our source for discernment and strategies of breakthrough.

A threatened demon might begin to name off other spirits that are present, or begin to cry in a way that makes you think the person receiving ministry is crying. I have even witnessed demons arguing over who will leave first because they do not want to forfeit their hold. It is important not to get sidetracked by these tactics, but to take authority over the manifestations and to stay focused on issuing the final eviction notice.

10. Pray until Freedom Comes

Webster's dictionary tells us that *freedom* is "liberation from the control of some other person or power." When true breakthrough has occurred, both the captive and the ministry team will know it. When demons take their leave, it is usually evident that they have been cast out successfully.

Some deliverance issues require a great deal of ministry time. It is not unusual for ministry to take several sessions, each lasting two to three hours. In between ministry sessions, the one seeking prayer has to press in and war in order to overcome the demonic stronghold. In these instances I stay in close communication with the one receiving ministry, making myself available to pray over the phone and counsel as necessary.

There are times when freedom is realized several days after a ministry session. I prayed for a pastor while on an altar ministry team. He was bound by a spirit of pride and was more than ready for freedom. As our team ministered, the pastor began to receive liberty, but we were unable to get the final breakthrough. I explained that he would have to press into the Lord to crowd out that spirit of pride. We left him with instructions to follow after returning home. He was to audibly read Scriptures that spoke of his identity in Christ, spend time in worship before the Lord and begin to make correct decisions and choices of humility. Four days later I received the report that the spirit of pride had left and this wonderful man of God was free.

Once a demon has been evicted, pray and ask the Lord if there are any other gateways to be dealt with. There could be more than one deceiving spirit at work. As I have shared, there is no exact model for deliverance ministry. As we listen to the Holy Spirit, each ministry setting will take on its own model of prayer.

Often the one receiving prayer will have to choose to renounce the demonic stronghold in order to gain complete freedom. It is also helpful sometimes to read the Word of God and worship during ministry sessions.

11. Be Aware of the Need for Inner Healing

Let's return to Candy. She was raised in a home that was very unstable. Not only did she need deliverance ministry, but also prayers of inner healing. I have mentioned inner healing several times. *Inner* simply refers to the more intimate or secret state of the mind or spirit. *Healing* means to make sound or healthy or to get rid of troubles or grief. I define *inner healing*, then, as the process of partnering with the Lord to cleanse the intimate and secret places of the mind, will and emotions from troubles and grief. It focuses on healing deep wounds in our minds and emotions that hinder emotional and spiritual well-being.

Inner healing is usually related to repeated and devastating breaches of trust with someone who is close. It is also needed following a traumatic or violating event, or when a loved one should and could have given protection but did not. In my experience, deliverance and inner healing go hand in hand to provide complete healing and restoration.

After evicting the demons that grip someone like Candy following devastating childhood experiences, I lead the person in a time of inner healing. I ask the Lord to heal and wash over his or her emotions and memories with His acceptance, love and peace, inviting His restoration. I also ask the Lord to bring a new and fresh impartation and revelation of His love.

It is wonderful to witness the healing power of the touch of God. Are the painful memories forgotten? Usually not, but the sting of the memories will be gone, and the emotions will be made whole once more. Candy will be able to love and trust freely and will no longer experience a barrier in her relationship with her heavenly Father.

12. Fill the House with the Holy Spirit

Once a spirit has been successfully cast out and the house swept clean, it is vital to ask the Holy Spirit to fill all the empty and void places.

> "When an evil spirit comes out of a man, it goes through arid places seeking rest and does not find it. Then it says, 'I will return to the house I left.' When it arrives, it finds the house unoccupied, swept clean and put in order. Then it goes and takes with it seven other spirits more wicked than itself, and they go in and live there. And the final condition of that man is worse than the first."
>
> Matthew 12:43–45

Sandra had submitted herself to deliverance and inner healing. After several weeks, she had received great breakthrough, but she continued to feel that there was still a final deception to be conquered.

During this time of ministering to Sandra, she shared that her mother had passed away over a year ago and had left her house to Sandra. Since Sandra had her own home, she listed her mother's house with a real estate agent. It had been on the market for a year, and seven contracts had fallen through. Even the agent expressed concern that something was not right. We scheduled a time for a ministry team to meet at the house.

First, we walked the property, breaking all defilement off the land. As we made our way into the home, the presence of evil was quite evident. Sandra's mother had practiced witchcraft, and the presence of evil still lingered in the dark, musty, vacant rooms.

Sandra took us into her childhood room. It felt cold and damp, and there was a powerful sense of death and evil. We knew that the property was the site of betrayals and murders of Native Americans, including women and children. During her youth, Sandra had encountered numerous demonic visitations of dead Indian spirits and developed a strong spiritual bond with them. I knew that this was the last issue to be dealt with in order for Sandra to have complete freedom.

We prayed, breaking all ties between Sandra and the spirits on the land. As the command was issued, Sandra began to weep tears of joy. She knew that her captivity was over. The other team members and I laid hands on her, inviting the Holy Spirit to fill all the empty and void places in her life. As we did, Sandra received her prayer language and began to laugh with joy. To seal this day of victory, the Lord miraculously touched Sandra's eyes. We watched as they were transformed from a pale green to a bright crystal blue!

Within a week a contract was placed on the property, and it sold for the asking price without any complications or delays. Sandra received her rightful inheritance. Our God is an amazing, all-powerful, delivering God.

13. Speak Prayers of Replacement

One of the final actions I take in deliverance ministry is to speak forth life-giving purposes that are opposite in nature to the evil lies the demons have established. In Candy's situation, I prayed like this:

> Lord, thank You for freedom and deliverance in Candy's life. We rejoice in Your goodness and faithfulness to her. Lord, we thank You that she will never be the same again. Lord, we speak life where there has been death, boldness where there has been fear, acceptance and love where there has been rejection, and abounding joy where there has been depression. Lord, allow all Your blessings to flow forth out of Candy. May she be filled to overflowing with Your spirit and presence. Lord, we declare that this is a new day for our sister in Christ. The grave clothes have been shed. She is a free daughter of the King.

14. Seal the Work by the Blood of the Lamb

All rulers have a "signet," a device that marks documents as official. It is often worn as a ring on the finger. The blood of Jesus is the "signet ring" of the One who defeated all powers of darkness. It is His blood that serves as a stamp or seal of approval of the completed work and newfound freedom. This seal becomes a barrier between the natural and the demonic realm that cannot be penetrated unless permission or access is given.

In closing with Candy, I prayed:

Lord, we now ask that You seal the work that has been done in Candy's life by the blood of the Lamb, serving as a sign to all that she is free and that the demons no longer have access to her. It is in Jesus' name that we pray. Amen.

Is Freedom Always Achieved?

Throughout our study, we have viewed many stories of incredible breakthrough and freedom. God is faithful and moves on behalf of His children. Still, there are times in ministry, even with experienced teams, that victory is not achieved. There are a number of reasons for this.

Sometimes the person asking for prayer really does not desire freedom. Sadly enough, there are many individuals who enjoy the attention that their problems bring and do not want to let go of it. In this instance every opportunity for deliverance should be presented. The team needs to explain to the individual that the Lord desires freedom for him or her, but he or she has to want it. It cannot be forced. If the person still chooses to embrace the demonic issue, then the session must be ended with an understanding that ministry will not resume until the person asking for ministry is truly ready for spiritual breakthrough.

In other instances a team member may be struggling with the same issue the ministry team is trying to break off the captive. The two spirits feed off each other, increase in strength and hinder complete freedom. In this circumstance, the team member should be asked to leave the room for the rest of the session. Following the session, the team leader should share the discernment with the team member and pray for him or her. All of this should be done with care and courtesy. Remember that a leader's role is to build up and never to tear down.

Sometimes we simply do not have the answers or the anointing to handle the situation. If breakthrough is not achieved, I refer the person to another deliverance ministry that I know has expertise and anointing.

Remember, in the Body of Christ we need each other and should never come to the decision that our way is the only way. We must maintain a position of humility and be open to the fact that someone else might have the solution. On the other hand, we should never be afraid to tackle new arenas in deliverance ministry. If we refuse to let go of the status quo, then our anointing will not increase and our ministry will soon be dormant. We have to be willing to risk in the anointing of the Holy Spirit. This is how we grow in Him.

11

WALKING IN FREEDOM

And show your own self in all respects to be a pattern and a model of good deeds and works, teaching what is unadulterated, showing gravity [having the strictest regard for truth and purity of motive], with dignity and seriousness.

Titus 2:7, AMP

The ministry session is almost completed. The demons have been evicted, and the recipient of prayer is no longer bound by darkness. Now one final step remains: Before leaving the ministry time, you will need to explain to the recipient how to maintain the victory.

Why is this necessary? Because the demons will try to regain entrance. They will attempt to snare the prayer recipient, and they will use temptation as bait. If the ministry recipient understands this demonic tactic, however, two things happen. One, the recipient does not have to endure

177

the questioning and confusion of wondering whether or not the breakthrough was real; and, two, he or she is prepared and equipped to stand against future attacks.

You need to know, however, that even with preparation, the battle to maintain victory will be difficult—and some you minister to will fail. It is tragic when a person who has been set free allows himself or herself to be lured into the trap of deception. Let me give you an example.

Before coming to salvation, John had been actively involved in a satanic coven. He was steeped in evil rituals that invited demons into his physical body. He spent many nights in a cemetery sleeping inside crypts on top of coffins, hoping to gain evil power from the departed who had led ungodly, evil lives. He and the other coven members were heavy drug users and spent the majority of their free time high on drugs.

But John had a praying family who would not give up on him. Gradually the prayers began to have a powerful effect. For years his parents had faithfully invited John to church, and one day he accepted. He went to church and got saved that night. Within several weeks, he was baptized and began his new journey in the Lord.

That was not the end of his battle with darkness, however. John had made pacts with demons, and they did not want to give up their hold. He was just in his late twenties but began suffering from a severe case of diabetes. His life was in danger, and the doctors did not give a good prognosis. John had heard of deliverance ministry and contacted me for prayer.

Over a period of several weeks, the team ministered to John. He received great freedom, and his health began to improve. We gave him instruction and provided accountability in walking out his freedom as we ministered to him. He was given homework assignments of reading the Bible, spending time in prayer and worshiping. He also became actively involved in a Bible study with men his age. He was doing well, and we were all excited about the progress we saw in his life.

In our last ministry session with John, one of the team members told him that she felt the Lord wanted to give him a warning. Here is what she said: "John, I feel that you need to be cautious of a past relationship trying to come into your life again. Even if you think you can stand, the temptation will prove to be a difficult trap to turn away from. Do not revisit old friendships and evil habits of the past."

John responded positively to this directive from the Lord and agreed to be on guard. We made ourselves available to John; anytime he needed prayer or support he was free to contact us. I made several follow-up phone calls to check on him and to get a report of his progress in the Lord. He seemed to be on the right track.

Then one day I received disturbing news. John was found in his apartment in a deep diabetic coma. I learned that he had begun to spend time with his former best friend who was still actively involved in drugs and Satanism. Within a short time, John had been drawn back into drugs. The men in his Bible study had attempted to reach out to John, but he had stopped returning their phone calls. The day he was found he was lying in the center of a formation of lit candles, attempting to reengage in a satanic ritual. My heart breaks for John as he is still in a battle for his life.

If John had truly been set free, then why was he pulled back into this evil and not able to maintain the victory? The answer lies in the power of choice and exercising this right in a righteous and godly fashion. Self-discipline means doing the right things even when our flesh and emotions dictate otherwise. The Bible teaches this:

> Physical training is of some value (useful for a little), but godliness (spiritual training) is useful and of value in every-

thing and in every way, for it holds promise for the present life and also for the life which is to come.

1 Timothy 4:8, AMP

The truth is that spiritual training and discipline lead to godliness, and godliness helps us walk in freedom and blessing—in this life and the next. That is the primary message that you will want to impart to someone who is completing deliverance ministry. Those who truly walk in freedom are honest and sincere with pure motives. They are not self-seeking and are characterized by hearts drawn to model love and good deeds of the Father. Then when temptation comes, the person who has been set free remains free.

Final Responsibilities of the Ministry Team

Deliverance ministry involves not only praying and releasing the captive from the grip of darkness but also walking with the person through the process of complete victory. Here are other important points for you to review as you draw the ministry session to a close. We have discussed several of these; they are part of the vibrant Christian life.

Fellowship with Other Believers

You cannot stress enough with ministry recipients the importance of being in relationship and fellowship with other believers. Being active in a church or corporate gathering on a regular basis aids spiritual development and well-being. Living independently leaves people with little or no room to hear new and challenging truths from the Word of God. It also keeps them in a place of isolation, allowing more of an opportunity for spiritual laziness. Once lazy and passive, they are no longer guarding the anointing in their lives. This, in turn, unlocks a door that the demonic will use to regain entrance.

Accountability Relationships

Hand in hand with fellowship is some form of spiritual accountability. I am not talking about relationships that dictate every move. I am speaking of those associates and friends who have been given the right to speak into the ministry recipients' lives. These are people they choose to walk with and share life experiences with. They are the friends who love them enough to pray with them through the difficult times and speak truth into their lives when needed. Building these types of relationships and remaining teachable helps to guard against deception.

Time in the Word of God

Those who are concluding deliverance ministry must be open to letting the light of Scripture shine in their lives. Look at the supernatural ability it has to keep their thoughts and motives in check:

> For the Word that God speaks is alive and full of power [making it active, operative, energizing, and effective]; it is sharper than any two-edged sword, penetrating to the dividing line of the breath of life (soul) and [the immortal] spirit, and of joints and marrow [of the deepest parts of our nature], exposing and sifting and analyzing and judging the very thoughts and purposes of the heart.
>
> Hebrews 4:12, AMP

The Word of God is quick, alive, powerful and active. It is a double-edged sword. It will reach down into all parts and functions of ministry recipients' beings and pass verdicts. It will penetrate to the innermost secrets that are hidden from their consciousness and from the eyes and ears of other people. Time in the Word must be a priority for someone who is serious about maintaining freedom.

Time in Worship

Spending time worshiping the Lord will help ministry recipients rise above the circumstances of life and into the Lord's glorious presence. It is in the intimate place of worship where they will be able to quiet their souls, get their emotions under the authority of their spirits and hear the voice of the Lord. Worship gives believers the strength to press forward and move ahead in the peace of the Lord. It gives the assurance of freedom and victory.

Time in Prayer

Along with Scripture reading and worship, ministry recipients will need to develop a prayer life if they have not yet done so. Prayer is what secures their identities in the Lord and assures His protection. It helps them draw closer to God and see His desires and plans for their lives. It is in this place that spiritual transformation occurs, causing them to become a reflection of who He is. Prayer also gives them the confidence to stand in the midst of trial, temptation and attacks of the enemy.

Taking Every Thought Captive

I believe the last area to be conquered involves the patterns that develop in one's thought life. These processes are hidden and secret and, therefore, easy to conceal.

Scripture says to be strong in this regard: "We demolish arguments and every pretension that sets itself up against the knowledge of God, and we take captive every thought to make it obedient to Christ" (2 Corinthians 10:5). If a ministry recipient finds that his or her thoughts are contrary to the Word of God and His promises, then the door that entertains the unhealthy ideas needs to be shut.

How does he or she do that? Remind the recipient of how telephone marketers hope to invade his or her life! They know every trick for inducing the person on the other end of the line to purchase whatever product they are selling. Most people find that the only way to handle telemarketers is not to answer the phone. Some people use caller ID, some let the answering machine take the call—whatever works. If the marketer has the slightest opportunity to start his or her sales pitch, it gets harder and harder to hang up the phone.

The same is true with thoughts placed in the mind by demonic spirits. The person did not ask for those thoughts to come. He or she does not want them. The person must, therefore, not pick up the receiver and entertain the sales pitch. He or she needs to block the message from getting through and command it to stop coming in Jesus' name.

Sometimes the thoughts a person entertains are not demonic in origin but a product of his or her own fleshly desires. If people encourage thoughts that are focused on ungodly activities or that feed secret fantasy lives in their minds, then they are walking in sin. Jesus said: "But I tell you that anyone who looks at a woman lustfully has already committed adultery with her in his heart" (Matthew 5:28). Any kind of ungodly fantasy thought life needs to be renounced and repented of. Otherwise the enemy will take full advantage of the opportunity.

Making Things Right

Sometimes the ministry recipient will need to make restitution to walk in complete freedom. If sin was involved that harmed another individual, it most likely needs to be made right. Are there financial obligations that have not been met? These need to be paid. Not all things can be corrected, but if the Lord is consistently reminding the ministry recipient of something that needs to be rectified, it is important to obey.

Spiritual Housecleaning

Demons will attach themselves to inanimate objects. As part of deliverance ministry, all items associated with past ungodly relationships or activities should be thrown out or destroyed. Jewelry, clothing—any gift that was given from a relationship that produced ungodly soul ties has to be removed.

Advise the recipient to go through his or her home and throw out items that would be stumbling blocks. Movies, music, books and magazines that include pornography, strong sexual overtones or witchcraft, as just a few examples, are sure open doors to the demonic. Neither should small idols and icons purchased as souvenirs from a trip take up residence in his or her home. Much southwestern Native American art, for instance, has strong spiritual significance. Many times those making items such as dream catchers invite spirits to attach themselves to the finished product. Thus, when the item is brought into the home, darkness is also welcomed in.

I go through my home once a year. During this time I pray and listen to the leading of the Holy Spirit. If I sense I should get rid of an object, I do.

Follow-up Plans

And finally, as the team leader, I make myself available for prayer, encouragement and counseling as needed. I always check on the individual with follow-up phone calls.

Oftentimes after receiving freedom, an individual will desire to be discipled in deliverance ministry. I will invite the individual to be involved in my ministry at an appropriate level of training and equipping.

Exercising Our Spiritual Authority

Now that freedom has been realized, the recipient of deliverance ministry has newfound authority to exercise over the schemes of darkness in his or her life. This new power requires faith—and remember that faith is an unquestioning belief that does not require proof or evidence. When the demons attempt to retake their hold, it is time to exercise the believer's prerogative and command them to go in Jesus' name.

I told this story in my book *Authority to Tread*, but I want to repeat it here because it reveals my own battle with standing in authority over darkness and helps demonstrate how to stand in victory.

When my sister and I were children, we were staying at a childcare facility near our home while our parents went to a Dallas Cowboys football game with friends. She was six years old; I was three. While climbing on the monkey bars, I fell and broke my elbow. Cell phones did not exist at this time, so the caretaker was unable to reach my parents. I continued to cry uncontrollably, and she was unable to calm me.

Frustrated, she placed me in a crib in a dark room and refused to allow my distraught sister to be with me. I still remember my sister standing in the doorway of the room, wanting to come to me and not being allowed to do so. I was in pain and frightened. Needless to say, when my parents arrived to pick us up they were not happy, and we never stayed there again.

As a result of that incident, I became terrified of heights and the dark. From that time until I was delivered from fear as an adult, I was plagued with nightmares. Even after Greg and I were married and had our first child, fear had a grip on me. If he was traveling out of town on business, I could not sleep unless the television, radio and every light in the house were on. When I traveled by plane, I had to take enough Dramamine to put me to sleep. I could not stand ladders or balconies.

As the Lord began to teach me about intercession, deliverance and warfare, I realized I had to deal with these fears. How could I cast out a spirit of fear in another individual if I were walking in fear? How could I go to the places and nations the Lord was revealing to me in prayer if I were afraid of heights and flying? I began to cry out to the Lord for freedom. One time at a women's retreat, one of the speakers asked all of the women with fear issues to stand. He prayed over us corporately and broke the spirit of fear. I felt as if something perched on my shoulders left. I was thrilled!

When I returned home I knew I had been set free. Even so, I quickly learned that I was going to have to stand in my deliverance to keep the victory.

Every night for two months, I dealt with a spirit of fear. I could feel when the spirit would enter our home at night while we slept. Instead of burrowing my head under the covers or scooting closer to my husband for comfort, I would get out of bed, walk to the family room and address that spirit of fear. Even though I could not see it, I would walk to where I felt its presence the strongest and address it as if I were staring it in the eyes. I told it to leave in the name of Jesus and never come back. It was not welcome in my life or home any longer. I told fear that it would not touch my children or my husband.

During this time I spent many hours in the middle of the night praying. Even when I was worshiping the Lord and moving into intercession, that spirit of fear would try to return. I would rise from the floor and walk to the spot where I could feel the presence of fear and address it face-to-face.

Greg left town on a business trip. This was the true test! At night, after putting my daughter to bed, I turned off all the lights. The television and radio were off, and I proclaimed, "I am not submitting to fear any longer! I will not embrace you, spirit of fear!" Guess what? I was not afraid! Since that time, darkness and dark places do not bother me, and I have been able to fly without hesitation. But I had to stand to maintain the victory, and anyone being delivered from bondage will without a doubt need to stand to maintain his or her victory also.

In Closing

Scripture tells us that when we receive the Lord Jesus into our lives we become joint heirs with the Savior:

> And He raised us up together with Him and made us sit down together [giving us joint seating with Him] in the heavenly sphere [by virtue of our being] in Christ Jesus (the Messiah, the Anointed One).
>
> Ephesians 2:6, AMP

We are now identified in Him, and what belongs to Christ as the firstborn also belongs to us. Jesus has authority over all creatures, both in heaven and on earth. By His death on the cross Jesus defeated Satan and his army of darkness once and for all. As stated in 1 John 3:8, "The reason the Son of God was made manifest (visible) was to undo (destroy, loosen, and dissolve) the works the devil [has done]" (AMP).

It is our destiny and inheritance to walk in our blood-bought authority, partnering with the Lord in a life of freedom and victory. Along with those we will minister to, we no longer have to be held captive by dark lies and the schemes of demonic deception. The Lord has given us the ability to plunder the work of Satan in our lives. The kingdom of darkness will not prevail against us, for we are jointly seated with Jesus in the heavenly realms.

It is my prayer that *Breaking the Bonds of Evil* has helped equip and empower you to move forward in personal freedom. I pray that you have new confidence and authority to release prisoners from the chains that bind. I would like to close with this prayer for you:

> Father, I thank You for each brother and sister in Christ who is reading this book. I pray abundant blessings on each of them. Lord, may this be a new day of personal freedom and victory. And may it also be the beginning of a strategic season of newfound authority in You to release prisoners from their dark cells. May the anointing for breaking evil schemes and sharp, effective deliverance ministry be imparted now, in Jesus' name.
>
> Lord, bless their families and ministries. May all they put their hands to find the favor of the Lord, and may they enter this new day in the fullness of all You have called them to walk in.
>
> Thank You, Lord, for Your love and faithfulness. You are truly a good God. To You be all honor, glory and power. In Jesus' name I pray. Amen.

APPENDIX

The following is a list of cults and occult and witchcraft practices to use as a reference guide in deliverance ministry. This is not an exhaustive list. The Internet is a good resource for research. Also, two credible resources for in-depth discussions concerning practices centered on the occult and witchcraft are *The Occult Trap* by James S. Wallace and *Deliver Us from Evil* by Cindy Jacobs.

Some of these practices will be obvious, such as black magic. Some will be less obvious, such as a rosary, which is used to count prayers to Mary and dead saints and is superstitious in nature. And some may be unknown to you altogether, such as candomble, which is a South American witchcraft cult. It is important to be aware of these practices when praying for someone who has been steeped in them. Knowledge and understanding equip.

Altered states of consciousness
Amulets
Animal sacrifices
Ascended masters
Astral projection
Astrology

Auras

Avatar

Baha'i faith

Biofeedback

Black magic

Blood subscription

Book of Toth

Buddhism

Candomble

Centering

Chakras

Channeling

Charms

Christ consciousness

Christian Science

Clairvoyance

Crystal ball

Cybele

Demolay

Divination

Divining rod

Eastern religions

Eastern Star

Eighth through Thirteenth Books of Moses

ESP

Fantasy role-playing games like Dungeons and Dragons, Tunnels and Trolls and DragonQuest

Feng shui

Fetish

Fortune-telling

Freemasonry

Geomancy
Goddess worship
Hare Krishna
Harry Potter
Hinduism
Horoscopes
Hypnotism
Idolatry
Initiation ceremonies centered on pagan and demonic
    activities
Iridology
Islam
Jehovah's Witness
Job's Daughters
Kabbalah
Karma
Koran
Ku Klux Klan
Light as a feather
Love magic
Macumba
Magic
Mantras
Martial arts
Mediumism
Mind-altering drugs
Mormonism
Necromancy
Necronomicon
New Age cults
New Age meditation

Numerology
Occult movies
Omens
Ouija boards
Palm reading
Parapsychology
Pentagram
Pokèmon
Poltergeist
Psychic power
Pyramid power
Rebirthing
Reincarnation
Rosary beads
Rosicrucianism
Santeria
Satanic rock music
Satanism
Scientology
Séances
Shamanism
Shinto
Silva mind control
Sophia
Sorcery
Spirit guides
Spiritism
Superstition
Talisman
Taoism
Tarot cards

Tea-leaf reading
Telepathy
The Book of Changes (I Ching)
The Book of Shadows
Transcendental Meditation
Umbanda
Unitarianism
Voodoo
Water witching
White magic
Wicca
Witchcraft
Yoga
Zen
Zodiac

BIBLIOGRAPHY

Campbell, Ron. *Free from Freemasonry*. Ventura, Calif.: Regal, 1999.

Clark, Jonas. *Rejection Is Hell!* Hallandale, Fla.: Spirit of Life Publishing, 2002.

Damazio, Frank. *The Making of a Leader*. Portland, Ore.: Trilogy Productions, 1988.

Deere, Jack. *Surprised by the Voice of God*. Grand Rapids, Mich.: Zondervan, 1996.

Duggan, Dorman, with Frank Hammond. *The Strongman of Unbelief*. Plainview, Tex.: The Children's Bread Ministry, 2002.

Frangipane, Francis. *Discerning of Spirits*. Cedar Rapids, Iowa: Arrow Publications, 1991.

———. *Jezebel Spirit*. Cedar Rapids, Iowa: Arrow Publications, 1991.

———. *This Day We Fight: Breaking the Bondage of a Passive Spirit*. Grand Rapids, Mich.: Chosen, 2005.

———. *The Three Battlegrounds*. Marion, Iowa: Arrow Publications, 1989.

Gibson, Noel, and Phyl Gibson. *Evicting Demonic Intruders*. West Sussex, England: New Wine Press, 1993.

Hammond, Frank, and Ida Mae Hammond. *Pigs in the Parlor*. Kirkwood, Mo.: Impact Christian Books, 2004.

Hammond, Frank. *The Breaking of Curses*. Kirkwood, Mo.: Impact Christian Books, 1993.

———. *Comfort for the Wounded Spirit*. Kirkwood, Mo.: Impact Christian Books, 2000.

———. *Confronting Familiar Spirits*. Plainview, Tex.: Frank D. Hammond, 1995.

———. *Demons and Deliverance*. Kirkwood, Mo.: Impact Christian Books, 1991.

———. *Forgiving Others*. Plainview, Tex.: Frank D. Hammond, 1995.

———. *A Manual for Children's Deliverance*. Kirkwood, Mo.: Impact Christian Books, 1996.

———. *Overcoming Rejection*. Kirkwood, Mo.: Impact Christian Books, 1987.

———. *The Perils of Passivity*. Plainview, Tex.: Frank D. Hammond, 2004.

———. *Soul Ties*. Rev. ed. Plainview, Tex.: Frank D. Hammond, 1995.

Hayward, Chris. *God's Cleansing Stream*. Ventura, Calif.: Regal, 2003.

Heidler, Robert. *Restoring Your Shield of Faith*. Ventura, Calif.: Regal, 2004.

———. *Set Yourself Free*. Denton, Tex.: Glory of Zion International Ministries, 2002.

Horrobin, Peter. *Healing through Deliverance: The Foundation of Deliverance Ministry*. Grand Rapids, Mich.: Chosen, 2003.

———. *Healing through Deliverance: The Practice of Deliverance Ministry*. Grand Rapids, Mich.: Chosen, 2003.

———. *The Most Powerful Prayer on Earth*. Ventura, Calif.: Regal, 2004.

Jackson, John Paul. *Buying and Selling the Souls of Our Children*. Ft. Worth, Tex.: Streams Publications, 2000.

Jacobs, Cindy. *Deliver Us from Evil*. Ventura, Calif.: Regal, 2001.

———. *Possessing the Gates of the Enemy*. Grand Rapids, Mich.: Chosen, 1991.

———. *The Voice of God*. Ventura, Calif.: Regal, 1995.

Kylstra, Chester, and Betsy Kylstra. *Biblical Healing and Deliverance*. Grand Rapids, Mich.: Chosen, 2005.

———. *Restoring the Foundations*. Hendersonville, N.C.: Proclaiming His Word, 2000.

Murphy, Ed. *The Handbook for Spiritual Warfare*. Nashville, Tenn.: Thomas Nelson, 1992.

Nee, Watchman. *Changed into His Likeness*. Wheaton, Ill.: Tyndale, 1978.

———. *The Latent Power of the Soul*. Richmond, Va.: Christian Fellowship Publishers, 1972.

———. *Spiritual Authority*. Richmond, Va.: Christian Fellowship Publishers, 1972.

Pierce, Chuck, and John Dickson. *Worship Warrior*. Ventura, Calif.: Regal, 2002.

Pierce, Chuck, and Rebecca Wagner Sytsema. *The Future War of the Church*. Ventura, Calif.: Regal, 2001.

———. *Prayers That Outwit the Enemy*. Ventura, Calif.: Regal, 2004.

———. *Protecting Your Home from Spiritual Darkness*. Ventura, Calif.: Regal, 2000.

———. *When God Speaks*. Colorado Springs, Colo.: Wagner Publications, 2003.

Prince, Derek. *Blessing or Curse: You Can Choose*. Grand Rapids, Mich.: Chosen, 1990.

———. *They Shall Expel Demons*. Grand Rapids, Mich.: Chosen, 1998.

———. *War in Heaven*. Grand Rapids, Mich.: Chosen, 2003.

Sandford, John Loren, and Paula Sandford. *The Transformation of the Inner Man*. Clarks Summit, Pa.: Victory House, 1982.

Sherrer, Quinn, and Ruthanne Garlock. *The Spiritual Warrior's Prayer Guide*. Ann Arbor, Mich.: Servant, 1992.

———. *A Woman's Guide to Breaking Bondages*. Ann Arbor, Mich.: Servant, 1994.

Smith, Alice. *Beyond the Lie: Finding Freedom from the Past*. Minneapolis, Minn.: Bethany House, 2006.

———. *Beyond the Veil*. Ventura, Calif.: Regal, 1996.

———. *Delivering the Captives: How to Help Others Find Freedom in Christ.* Minneapolis, Minn.: Bethany House, 2006.

Smith, Eddie. *Breaking the Enemy's Grip.* Minneapolis, Minn.: Bethany House, 2004.

Smith, Eddie, and Alice Smith. *Discerning the Climate of the City.* Houston, Tex.: SpiriTruth, 1997.

———. *Dispelling the Darkness.* Houston, Tex.: SpiriTruth, 1998.

———. *Spiritual Housecleaning.* Ventura, Calif.: Regal, 2003.

Sorge, Bob. *Envy, the Enemy Within.* Ventura, Calif.: Regal, 2003.

Stevens, Selwyn. *Compromise, the Church and Freemasonry.* Wellington, New Zealand: Jubilee Resources, 2001.

———. *Masonic Symbolism Explained.* Wellington, New Zealand: Jubilee Resources, 1997.

———. *Unmasking Freemasonry.* Wellington, New Zealand: Jubilee Resources, 1999.

Sudduth, Bill. *Deliverance Training Manual.* Pensacola, Fla.: RAM Inc., 2000.

———. *So Free!* Pensacola, Fla.: RAM Inc., 2002.

———. *What's Behind the Ink?* Pensacola, Fla.: RAM Inc., 2004.

Thompson, Joseph. *I'm a Christian So How Can I Have a Demon?* Colorado Springs, Colo.: Yeshua Ministries, 2002.

Wagner, C. Peter. *Acts of the Holy Spirit.* Ventura, Calif.: Regal, 2000.

———. *Breaking Strongholds in Your City.* Ventura, Calif.: Regal, 1993.

———. *Churches That Pray.* Ventura, Calif.: Regal, 1993.

———. *Confronting the Powers.* Ventura, Calif.: Regal, 1996.

———. *Confronting the Queen of Heaven.* Colorado Springs, Colo.: Wagner Publications, 1998.

———. *Discover Your Spiritual Gifts.* Ventura, Calif.: Regal, 2002.

———. *Engaging the Enemy.* Ventura, Calif.: Regal, 1991.

———. *Freedom from the Religious Spirit.* Ventura, Calif.: Regal, 2005.

―――. *Hard Core Idolatry*. Colorado Springs, Colo.: Wagner Publications, 1999.

―――. *Humility*. Ventura, Calif.: Regal, 2002.

―――. *Prayer Shield*. Ventura, Calif.: Regal, 1992.

―――. *Praying with Power*. Ventura, Calif.: Regal, 1997.

―――. *The Queen's Domain*. Colorado Springs, Colo.: Wagner Publications, 2000.

―――. *Warfare Prayer*. Ventura, Calif.: Regal, 1992.

―――. *What the Bible Says about Spiritual Warfare*. Ventura, Calif.: Regal, 2001.

―――. *Your Spiritual Gifts Can Help Your Church Grow*. Ventura, Calif.: Regal, 1992.

Wagner, Doris. *How to Cast Out Demons*. Ventura, Calif.: Renew, 2000.

―――. *How to Minister Freedom*. Ventura, Calif.: Renew, 2000.

Wallace, James S. *The Occult Trap*. Colorado Springs, Colo.: Wagner Publications, 2004.

INDEX

201